# *Twice Convicted*

*Philip J. Cebula*

**Twice Convicted**





---

*Cover photograph by Peter Plastridge*

---

***All Scripture quotations are taken from the New International Version (NIV) Bible***

*ISBN 978-0-615-62381-8*
*Library of Congress Control Number 2012909419*

*Printed in the USA by*
*Morris Publishing®*
*3212 E. Highway 30*
*Kearney, NE 68847*
*800-650-7888*
*www morrispublishing.com*

# Dedications

*I dedicate this book to*
*my lovely wife Irene,*
*who has stood by my side*
*throughout the years.*

*She is without challenge, my best friend,*
*my fountain of encouragement*
*and my model of Christianity.*
*Her unwavering support in the writing of*
*this book has brought its pages to fruition.*

*And to my late parents,*
*Felix and Irene Cebula*
*who raised me the proper way,*
*and loved me when I went astray.*

# Endorsements

*"A wonderful, inspiring testimony of a life changed by the saving power of Jesus Christ! The Lord has touched many lives through Pastor Phil's life and story, including my own Call into a lifetime of prison ministry!* ***Twice Convicted*** *is a must read for anyone seeking a true life change."*

**Tom Kurtz, Massachusetts State Prison Chaplain 20+ years**
*Tom also pastors* ***C****ross* ***P****oint Christian Church in Oxford, MA.*

---

*"Pastor Phil's dedication to the Word of God and his inspiring testimony of* ***Twice Convicted*** *is a Door of Hope for the lost. Many have been touched through his ministry and have gone on to serve the Lord. Upon entering prison, 13 doors clanged shut behind him, but he didn't give up, finding out that "He (who) will open up those doors" did so for him. His ministry continues to bring hope to those incarcerated with a guilty verdict of death through sin to everlasting life. Are you ready?"*

**Rev. Esther Kerry Plastridge, Branches of the Vine, Jacksonville, FL.** *(Missions Outreach)*

---

***"Twice Convicted*** *gives us a glimpse of what the Holy Spirit can do to change a man who is broken, making him a new creation full of hope and the grace of God. Pastor Phil is a lover of Jesus who has allowed the Lord to use him for His Glory. Read and see! The Lord is still doing mighty works in these last days."*

**Pastor John Konieczko, Pilgrim Covenant Church, Lunenburg, MA.**

---

*"DO IT NOW! - WHY WAIT? - Words spoken to Phil Cebula inside the walls of the Attica Prison.* ***Twice Convicted*** *compels us to look beyond our current problems and struggles to a life where one reaches incredible heights previously unimagined. - Read this book! DO IT NOW! - WHY WAIT?"*
**Lead Pastor Dave Tralongo**
**Chair City Community Church, Gardner, MA**

# Acknowledgments

*My children  Andrea, Jennifer, Daniel, & Cheryl,*
*who in many ways have sacrificed quality time with their father*
*as I fulfilled God's call on my life.+*

*Ernest J. Gaudet, his encouragement and suggestions for textual enhancements and loving critique are reflected in all its pages*

+

*Emy Vazquez, whose Sunday Morning sermon reminded me it was time to write this book.*

+

*Reverend Esther & Peter Plastridge,*
*who helped me see the bigger picture; the mission field*

+

*Eduardo & Maria Aponte, who opened up their home to Door of Hope Ministries*

+

*Reverend Normand Farrington,*
*My pastor behind the walls of Attica*

+

*Nancy McLaughlin and Curt Donahue*
*for their much needed proof-reading skills*

# *Table of Contents*

# *Table of Contents*

# *Introduction*

## (Author's Comments)

The intended purpose of "***Twice Convicted"*** is neither to glorify crime nor exploit man's sinful nature. Nor are its objectives to ignore and or minimize pain and suffering inflicted upon others. Its foremost purpose is for the reader to better understand the depth of God's love and His immeasurable forgiveness extended in the midst of very tragic circumstances.

"***Twice Convicted***" is the insightful story of my conviction in the court of justice, and my conviction before the throne of a sovereign and loving God. His tender mercies are indeed new every morning and His grace is sufficient.

***Philip J. Cebula***

*"But with you there is* ***forgiveness****, so that we can, with reverence, serve you." (Psalm 130:4)*

# Chapter One

## Early Years

*"Before I formed you in the womb I knew you,*
*before you were born I set you apart;*
*I appointed you as a prophet to the nations"*
(*Jeremiah 1:5*)

**M**y parents were good parents. They never would have dreamt that I would ever get so mixed up. I was born January 6, 1948 south of Buffalo in the Steel City of the Great Lakes, Lackawanna, New York. My early childhood was a typical boy growing up shoveling Buffalo snow and inhaling pollution from giant smoke stacks that shaped our skyline and filled the air with soot from the Bethlehem Steel Corporation. How often I remember the air sparkling with pollutants, never realizing how harmful the quality of air was to those who inhaled it with regularity. As you can imagine, cancer was king in Lackawanna. The "plant", as we called it, was the primary employer to most of the 25 thousand residents of our city. We were blue collar through and through. Moms stayed at home (toiling from sun up till sun down) while dads went to the "plant" carrying their black lunch boxes with 2 sandwiches and a glass thermos bottle inside. Being of Polish heritage our family was very Catholic and went to church every week. I took Catechism classes, made my First Holy Communion and Confirmation and learned how to "recite my prayers". (Now I lay me down to sleep.....) I would go to confession, say a good act of contrition, and be on my way, but you know how it is. It didn't take very long for me to sin again. And the recurring routine would start anew.

# *Twice Convicted*

Around my 14th year I began going to church without my parents. After all, I was old enough to make my own decisions, right? My friends and I would meet for "church" at the corner soda-shop; get together with a few girls and never make it to church. Little by little I was turning in another direction. Within a few years, my church going days were just about over, except for Christmas, Easter, funerals and weddings. Tradition is hard to break.

My high school graduation occurred in 1965 during the height of the Viet Nam War. The draft board was after me .........so I beat them to the punch, I volunteered for the draft in April of 1967 and by September of that year, still in my teens, I was dodging bullets, avoiding booby traps, and maneuvering airboats throughout the Mekong Delta of South Viet Nam. It was too late to burn my draft card and become a draft dodger. I was the property of the Unites States Army and they were teaching me so many important things about life; how to drink alcohol excessively, cuss, smoke marijuana, use drugs, gamble, and all that man stuff. Don't get me wrong. The Army also taught me plenty of good things that still have meaningful influence in my life

**Posing with captured weapons**

today, but a "sin nature" was inherent within me; often leading down the wrong path.

Unlike so many brave men and women that did not make it back alive, or came back maimed and disfigured, I survived the war, but I was not the same. Outwardly I appeared to be normal, but inwardly the war was still waging. Post Traumatic Stress Syndrome (PTS) wasn't diagnosed in those days and GI's were just left to deal with it without professional assistance. I don't think my level of PTS was severe but it was clearly affecting my behavior. Society needs to know that it doesn't take much PTS to influence one's life in a negative way. My desire for drugs and alcohol increased until one day in the spring of 1975 I found myself with a gun in my hand. I pulled the trigger and by the time the sun came up the next morning I was charged with murder. I made a lot of really bad choices and I needed HELP. I needed a change but I began to think that it was too late. Thank God, it's never too late.

# Chapter Two

## The Brick Wall

*"Watch and pray so that you will not fall into temptation. The spirit is willing, but the flesh is weak." (Mark 13:38)*

**C**risis was written all over my life in those early months of 1975. I was 27 years old and my life was snowballing downhill. There was always beer in my refrigerator and in my belly. I was secretively doing drugs and spending more time out of the house than in. I was laid off from working at the South Buffalo Railway, had my unemployment check in my hand and plenty of time to spend it in the wrong places. Most people, including myself, didn't understand what a jerk I was. I was rather popular; so I thought. My popularity led to enormous amounts of pride, and eventually pride led to destruction. *"Pride goes before destruction, a haughty spirit before a fall." (Proverbs 16:18)*

I fooled a lot of people but not my wife. One day she had enough of my antics. She packed up her bags and my cherished 2 year old daughter Andrea; slammed the door behind her and left. It wasn't the first time she left me. In my pride, I thought, "She'll be back." I was wrong, wrong, wrong. This time she came to her senses. She was gone for good. Our marriage eventually ended in divorce. When I look back at that time in my life, I also would have left me. It took me a long time to realize the error of my ways. Pride will always blind you from honest evaluation. From my haughtiness I peered down at everyone else.

No one knew I thought like this. I was a likable guy and wasn't going to jeopardize that image. So there I was, full of pride, money in my pocket, time on my hands and nothing to do. So what did I do? The drinking and the partying increased. The snow ball of destruction was gaining size and momentum. Time was running out and little did I know that I was only a few months away from hitting the proverbial brick wall. Lackawanna, New York had plenty of bars available if someone wanted to ruin their life. You could always find a place that served alcohol after hours. My favorite hangout for late night drinking was the ever popular *"My Place"* Family Restaurant. There was nothing family about it. It surely wasn't a restaurant unless you called selling beer nuts and pickled eggs a restaurant. But I loved it there. That's where my friends would hang out. That's where the other guys like me would be found. There was always plenty of booze, girls, pool, and "fellowship". In the summer the motorcycles would park outside; and inside the trash talk would take place. In the winter we would hope for one of those infamous Buffalo area snow storms to fall so we would have another excuse for not driving home in a blizzard.

It was now late May of 1975. My unemployment checks were still coming in and my lifestyle was unchanging. On this particular Friday night my drinking had continued into the early hours of Saturday. I was drinking a little more that night and had smoked a little marijuana. I'm not sure how it began but I found myself in an argument with some of my buddies at *"My Place"*. The proprietor/bartender said a guy was in earlier that night claiming to be my friend, and he was causing some kind of ruckus in his fine establishment. I was told to do my best to keep him from coming back again. I hardly knew this guy. We were neighbors but not necessarily good friends.

I continued to drink that night until approximately 3 o'clock in the morning. The bar finally closed and I went home. My buddy came with me. I reminded him that I had plenty of Budweiser in my refrigerator.

As we sat on my porch and had a few more beers, I decided to go next door to see this neighbor of mine who caused such a ruckus at "*My Place*". The truth was I wasn't so concerned that he caused trouble at the bar; I was more concerned that my name was brought up in the midst of it. Pride never likes to look like the bad guy and all the more so when bolstered with drugs and alcohol. At about 4 o'clock I got up from my porch chair and went charging into my neighbor's home (The door was not locked). I went into his bedroom, flipped on the light switch, stood beside his bed and gave him a piece of my mind. As he stood up I realized just how big and tall he was in comparison to me. After pushing and shoving each other for a few moments I shouted at him to, "Stay away from my hangouts." And I left.

"Have another beer" I said to my buddy as we continued to sit on my porch and talk trash. It was now about 30 minutes and a few beers later. It was still rather dark outside. The sun would soon be rising. As my friend and I discussed what happened, I looked to my right and noticed the lights go on next door. There was some noise coming out of the house, the screen door flew open, and he was coming down the sidewalk, heading my way. He wasn't happy. I don't blame him for being angry and I should have kept my distance but my judgment was greatly impaired by alcohol and drugs. I make no excuses. Drugs and alcohol cannot excuse me from what was about to happen in the next few minutes. Remember, pride is a destructive force and I was racing blindly toward the brick wall where it would all crash.

The street lights and the glowing moon lit up the area in front of my house just enough for me to see him coming. His shadow made him look 10 feet tall. He had a broad belt with a heavy buckle in his hand which he swung as he walked. I put my drink down on the porch railing, stood on my feet and looked his way as he continued to approach. He was about 25 feet away from me, still waving the belt and cursing as the distance rapidly shortened between us. I remember seeing that huge belt buckle reflecting in the moon light and I was sure its intended target was me.

Now charging toward me with slow deliberate heavy steps and glaring eyes he cursed me. I cursed him back! I realized I had created this sidewalk encounter when I was up in his bedroom and thought we had settled it. I thought the argument was over. I thought the bedroom fight had closure. I thought....I thought.... I thought. The truth was I didn't think. I said something like "Back off, I've had enough of you already." The air was charged with tension. I firmly believe an evil spirit was hovering over the immediate area. We cursed each other again, and as the gap shortened I knew that time was running out. I had to make a decision. He kept charging my way. The belt was swinging and the buckle was gaining centrifugal speed in search of me, its target. I should have run in the other direction but still under the influence of the alcohol, my judgment was tarnished.

Hurriedly I raced up the two steps, crossed my porch, opened my screen door and reached my hand into the nearby coat closet. In seconds I was back outside, standing on the sidewalk glaring back at him. But now I was holding a hunting rifle in my hand. I'll never know why I didn't lock the door and stay in the house.

I could have prevented what was about to happen but my drunken judgment was horrendously askew. A cloud of darkness was settling down in front of my house and I never knew it.

By then he was about ten feet from me; continuing to approach deliberately and still brandishing that belt. I lifted the rifle and pointed it in his direction. I was sure when he saw what I was holding he'd back off. I didn't have any intention of using it. I was bluffing. I never thought he would call my bluff. He swung the belt at me but I was able to duck and pull my head back enough. He missed. I pulled the trigger. Meanwhile my friend was still standing on the porch watching all this unfold. "What the #@!!% did you do? Did you shoot him? Did you hit him?" I knew I shot the rifle but I wasn't sure if I had hit him. We were rather close to each other, only a few feet apart, but I still wasn't sure if I had.

The gun had fired. He looked at me and cursed, and then walked back into his house. He didn't flinch, stagger, or appear to be in any pain or jeopardy. I remember standing there watching him as he made an about face and headed back into his house. "I guess I missed." I declared. I turned back to my friend and said, "Let's have another beer." At that moment darkness was over me to such an extent that it kept me from seeing the severity of what just took place. I think this is in part what Jesus meant when he said, *"See to it, then, that the light within you is not darkness." (Luke 11:35)*

It was now about 4:30 a.m. and we were sitting on my porch trying to unravel the events of the night. By now all the lights were on in the house next door. Even though their curtains were drawn we could see plenty of silhouette movement as people scurried about the house. I couldn't finish my beer. I seemed to be sobering up rapidly.

What happened? What did I do? Did I hit him? Was he alright? Do they need help? Should I run? I decided to call next door. "Hello, this is Phil. Is everything alright over there?" They hung up. I called again, "Hello, this is Phil. Do you need any help?" No voice on the other end, just CLICK. I called a third time and the response was no different. I called again and offered a ride to the hospital if necessary............they hung up again. I wasn't sure what happened. With all the commotion going on in their house I began to think he must be hurt. But why didn't he flinch or stagger? Why did he walk back into his house without revealing any degree of pain? If he was hit, wouldn't there be some blood on the sidewalk? If he was in danger, why didn't they call an ambulance? What was going on?

Finally at about 5 a.m., I said to my friend, "Let's get out of here". We got into my car and headed to a nearby coffee shop. We ordered coffee to go and went back to my car to drink it. The sun had broken through the dark sky and the birds were singing. As we sat there and sipped our coffee, fear began to take over. What do I do now? How can I find out if he's OK? My stomach was so nerved up that I couldn't drink the coffee. My buddy said, "Phil, take me home. This has been quite some night. I've got to sleep it off." I dropped him off, and now I sat there in my car, alone. I drove around for about an hour. It seemed like an eternity. When you are overwhelmed with trouble, "alone" is a frightening place to be. It's the place where fear can grip your soul and leave you despondent and depressed. "Alone" is a powerful tool of the enemy. What a person needs most when "alone" is to be with others, yet the spirit of "alone" will cause you to be withdrawn and separated from those you need the most. If you remain alone long enough you are in danger of being led to the door of suicide. Many victims of loneliness have walked through that door.

# *The Brick Wall*

Where do I go now? I drove around for a little while. I didn't know what to do next. Alone again.......I decided to visit my sister and brother-in-law. I remember driving the three or four miles to their house. While on my way I saw a couple police cars coming down the street in my direction. My heart started pounding. I thought surely they were after me. But they just drove past, my heart still pounding. Another mile, another squad car, but it had nothing to do with me. They were probably just making their routine runs. My heart was pumping so hard I could almost hear it.

By 6 a.m. I'm standing at my sister's front door. Knock-knock. Bob, my brother-in-law, greeted me at the door and I began to tell him the story of what happened. We talked a little bit over some coffee while my sister was just getting up. She told me that she was listening through her bedroom door to everything her husband and I talked about. While still in a half-sleep stupor she heard me say that I may have shot someone. She continued to eavesdrop from the bedroom and wondered if she was dreaming or did she really hear what she thought she heard? Bob and I have always been good friends and I needed a friend to talk to. We talked about 15-20 minutes. I realized I had to make an important decision. This time my problem did not have a simple solution. I had to turn myself in. My sister stayed at home with their two young children while Bob and I drove to the local police department. After we left she turned on the radio and heard the news bulletin, "There has been a shooting in the area and the police are looking for the suspect." She knew they were looking for me. The manhunt was on. It was 7 a.m. when we arrived at the police department headquarters. The officer at the front desk greeted me as I walked in. "Excuse me officer, I'm not sure, but I may have shot someone." The manhunt was over. I hit the brick wall.

# Chapter Three

## The Interrogation

*"A false witness will not go unpunished and whoever pours out lies will not go free."*
*(Proverbs 19:12)*

**B**ob and I walked into the station together yet I felt "alone". The officer at the desk was authoritative, yet polite, as he escorted me into the backroom so we could talk. Confused, tired, and afraid; I sat down. "Get yourself comfortable. We have just a few questions to ask. This shouldn't take very long." I didn't grasp the severity of the situation at hand even though they read me my Miranda rights. The questioning began. I was nervous on the inside, but on the outside I tried to look calm and confident (Probably more like cocky and arrogant). I'm sure I wasn't fooling anyone in the room, especially myself. "Go ahead" the officer said, "Tell us what happened. Tell us exactly how you remember it. Don't leave anything out. Relax. We've got plenty of time."

The interrogation began. It wasn't like I saw on TV. I wasn't sitting under a hot light as they blasted me with questions. The atmosphere was rather casual. They offered me a cigarette. "No thanks, I just quit." I was given a cup of coffee and then I began to talk. I didn't spill my guts like a scene from the movies. I just talked; they listened. They asked questions; I responded. Literally hours went by. One officer would say, "OK, I don't have any more questions." and he would leave the room as another would enter and begin his line of questioning. I don't remember how many people I spoke with that morning, but one after another they kept at me. I was honest with my answers but not completely. I was holding back information.

They asked me about the gun, where was it now, did I shoot it, was I alone, where was I earlier that night, how much did I drink.....and on and on the questions were asked and repeated and asked and repeated. The minutes turned into hours. They knew I was holding back from them. Partial truth is not truth at all. I wasn't getting anything over on them. They were going to continue grilling me until I spilled the necessary beans for them to either let me go or lock me up.

I was actually beginning to believe my half truths. I was getting confused in my own story. I couldn't remember what I said to them an hour or so earlier. My answers were beginning to contradict each other. The Scottish poet and historian Sir Walter Scott (1771-1832) penned it accurately when he wrote these words of truth, "Oh what a tangled web we weave, when first we practice to deceive." I had backed myself into a corner and didn't even know it (The brick wall again). I talked long enough. They had me! They had the information they needed. The interrogation was finally over. "Ok Phil, that's all the questioning for now. We'll be talking more at a later time". I remember thanking them for being easy on me. They thanked me for being cooperative. It was when I got up from my chair and began to leave the room that the officer in charge said, "I'm sorry Phil, but you won't be able to go today." I said, "Officer, I've told you everything I could remember (I was lying). I don't have anything more to say. I'm tired, I'm hungry, and I just want to go home. I'll be at home if you need me." Again the officer repeated himself, "Phil, you're not going home." When I said, "Why not?" that's when I heard the dreaded words, "Philip J. Cebula you are now under arrest for the murder of your neighbor." I couldn't believe my ears. It couldn't be true. This must be a nightmare. I was momentarily numb. My stomach ached, my head swirled, and my knees began to buckle. I was devastated by the charge. I wasn't expecting to hear this.

# The Interrogation

Up until that moment I didn't know he died. I wasn't even sure I had hit him. I remember how he walked so confidently back into his house. What had happened?

The officers left me alone for a moment as I went and gazed out the window at the trees, the birds, and blue skies. There was also a brick wall. It was there. No one else could see it, but I did. I saw it. It was there. By this time, my father had arrived and was waiting for permission to speak with me. They gave us a few private minutes together. I always got along with my dad and I was so glad to see him that day yet I had a difficult time looking his way because of my shame.

It was so awkward. I was glad to see him but I didn't want him to see me. I needed an embrace but I wanted to run and hide from him. I was hoping he would speak words of comfort, but I was afraid that all he could possibly say was there wasn't anything he could do for me. At first I looked down and turned my face away from him. Eventually our eyes met. It was a silent moment that ended with a tearful embrace. I remember saying "I'm sorry" and "I'm afraid." That's when he looked at me and said those three comforting words. "I love you." His voice seemed to quiver as he went on to say, "I want you to know that I'm here for you. I will do whatever I can to help you. I don't need to know what happened or how it happened. I'm not interested in knowing all that. Just know, my son, I'm here for you and we'll get through this somehow." After a short visit the officer came back and escorted me down the hall and into my room, a simple gray jail cell with toilet, small sink with only cold water, and a hard bed. **CLANG!!** The bars of my cell locked securely. I was terribly alone but my father's reassuring words of love were echoing in my mind; nurturing the heavy weight of my loneliness.

# Chapter Four

## The Man in the Mirror

*"As water reflects the face, so one's life reflects the heart." (Proverbs 29:11)*

How I ever ended up in a predicament like this I'll never understand. I was supposed to be most likely to succeed, not most likely to be behind bars. Many would have envied my upbringing. We didn't have much money but we were the ALL AMERICAN FAMILY, very close and dedicated to one another. My parents were children of Polish immigrants now living in the land of opportunity, but it was a time when very few opportunities existed. They survived the Great Depression only to be facing yet another crisis, World War II. By the time the war ended Felix Anthony Cebula had married Irene Florence Waryk and a new Cebula family was birthed into the world. My sister Diane was born December 8, 1946. I was second, January 6, 1948. Kathleen (Kathy) was born March 19, 1951. I find it ironic that today my sisters are both happily married to New York State Department of Corrections Officers. Mom and dad were great parents - no dysfunction in our house. The depression left them frugal and the war left them with a deep appreciation for our freedom. They never missed their opportunity to vote; a lesson of great value from the WWII generation.

**Kathy-Myself-Diane (1958)**

We were always doing something together as a family. Birthdays were celebrated, family vacations taken, and supper time together was seldom missed. Sunday always included church followed by Mom's home cooking. Sometimes if the weather was nice we would all jump into the family car for a "Sunday ride in the country." When we got home my dad would relax with a couple beers. He clearly didn't have any drinking problem; he simply enjoyed the taste of an ice cold beer. My mom would do the same; one small glass of beer was usually her limit. Life was good in the Cebula home. If my bike had a flat, Dad would fix it. If the house needed repairs, he'd repair it. Dad smoked about a pack a day and Mom might light up two or three times a week. She claimed she never inhaled. This was before the United States Surgeon General warned us of the dangers of smoking cigarettes. Family time was precious to my parents. If asked to work overtime, Dad would almost always refuse because he knew his time with the family was more valuable than having a few extra bucks. He showed me by his example that being frugal with your earnings will almost always leave you enough to enjoy the life you work so hard to enjoy.

Dad loved the outdoors and it was inevitable for us to become a camping family. In summer time Dad would pull into the driveway after work and we would all pitch in to pack up all the camping gear and head out for a weekend of camping. The state parks were usually our favorite places to camp, since they were less expensive and close by. There was always something going on in our family. Since I was the only boy I had favor when it came to spending time with Dad. Fishing and hunting were two sports we loved doing together. We always enjoyed spending time with each other. When I joined the Boy Scouts he supported me by becoming our Scoutmaster. My friends always told me how lucky I was to have my dad as the scoutmaster. Although I never told them, they were absolutely right.

# The Man in the Mirror

Our parents were always there when we needed them. Mom was the typical 1950's mom, washing clothes, ironing, cleaning house, preparing meals (no microwaves), and tucking us in for bed each night. As I got older I asked her to stop with the tucking. Hugs and kisses were rare in our home, and those three little words, I Love You, were seldom spoken yet never did I feel unloved.

**My Parents**

Many might deem in this a lack of parental warmth, but they could not be more mistaken. I wouldn't have traded my parents or my growing up experiences for anything. They were good parents and my home life was a joy. What caused me to go astray and end up behind bars is something I'll never fully grasp. It surely wasn't anyone else's fault. I wasn't raised that way. The greatest dilemma I could have ever posed to my parents was now upon us and their demonstration of love could not have been more profound and stalwart. With no other options available, my parents elected to strip their meager savings as well as placing a second lien against their home to provide money for my legal costs which would be considerable. My parents at that time, and for the rest of their lives, never brought up the subject of money or the great sacrifice that they had made for me. Of course my biggest problem was not about money. My number one problem was the man in the mirror. This whole gigantic crisis, burdensome to so many others, never should have happened. *"So then, each of us will give an account of himself to God."* (Romans 14:12)

# Chapter Five

## Could this be the WAY?

*"Jesus answered, I am the way, and the truth, and the life." (John 14:6a)*

Mug shots and fingerprints were taken. I was officially booked then stripped of my civilian clothes and given a jail outfit to wear. They took away my belt and shoelaces and made sure that I wasn't left with anything that I could use to harm myself. At one point during the booking process I stood stripped of everything and absolutely naked before them. They did a thorough inspection of my body for hidden contraband. I opened my mouth and they looked inside. I lifted my arms and they inspected my arm pits. I lifted my feet and they checked the bottoms for possible drugs taped to the bottom. They checked my scalp to see if anything was hidden in my hair. My mind was swirling constantly in unbelief. Time seemed to be at a stand-still. Every waking thought would replay the events of that dreadful night. I tried to sleep it off but that didn't work. Sometimes I would drift off for a little while only to awaken to the hard fact that couldn't be denied. I was in jail and about to face the most difficult days of my life.

Unknown to me my parents were frantically searching for an attorney. How do you find a good criminal attorney? Do you use the yellow pages? Do you make random phone calls to law offices in your area? How do you know if they are as good as they say? My parents had never been faced with a challenge like this before but eventually they selected one.

Early the next morning he came to the jailhouse to discuss the charges and the strategies he had for me. He only stayed about 20 minutes. He talked about a probable cause hearing, an official arraignment, and a bail hearing meeting that I would soon be facing. He shook my hand and left. I wasn't sure what he talked about. All his jargon left me confused. I thought he was there to help me. Why couldn't he get me released? I still hadn't grasped the severity of what I was facing.

After spending two days in the West Seneca jail, it was now time for me to be transferred. My arms were put in handcuffs and my feet wrapped in shackles as the officers prepared me for prisoner transfer. With chains dragging on the pavement I awkwardly shuffled my feet along as I was escorted to the police car that would transport me to the Erie County Holding Center in Buffalo, New York. After a fifteen-minute ride we arrived at the county jail. Again I was escorted into the center and the booking process was repeated; a stripped down body search, contraband inspection, mug shots, fingerprints, and the whole humiliating routine. Within an hour I was taken up the elevator and placed in my new "home", as they called it, and was told to get ready for my hearing. How do you get ready for an arraignment hearing? Will I be asked questions? I was several days unshaven, my hair was a mess, I needed a shower and my jail outfit didn't fit.

It was now late morning, my cell bars were opened and I was escorted down the hall and into an elevator to the basement level. We entered the "tunnel" that led to the courthouse. My attorney and a few members of my family were there as I entered the courtroom. My parents looked heartbroken as they peered my way; seeing their son wearing handcuffs and shackles. I was so consumed by my situation I never gave thought to their feelings. In addition to what I was putting my family through, my grandmother was terminally sick and only days away from her death.

# Could this be the Way?

Keep in mind this was not my trial; it's called a grand jury hearing. The purpose would be to determine whether or not there was enough probable cause to hold me. This arraignment would define the offense (if any) with which they would formally charge me. It didn't take very long. Within a few minutes it was official and I was charged with $2^{nd}$ degree murder and remanded back to the County Jail Holding Center to await trial. My defense attorney and the state's prosecuting district attorney would meet together with the judge and determine the best date for the trial to begin. My attorney said a few words to me........and off I went, back into the tunnel, up the elevator and into my cell. Thus began the longest thirty day period of my life.

County jail (the Bucket) time is uniquely different. It is the place where you are locked up while you await your day in court. The courtrooms of our country are bottle necked with cases waiting to be heard. Backed-up courts often hinder a person from getting a fair and speedy trial. At other times justice is delayed because of appointment conflicts between judges, district attorneys, and defense lawyers. It's not uncommon for someone to be held in the county jail for a year or longer. It's the place where day after day you are waiting for your day in court. You are locked in a cell for the bulk of the day. There is very little to do with your time; a little reading, some TV privileges, and a whole lot of time to think about why you're locked up. It's in this place of limbo that many have chosen suicide as their means of escape. Although suicide was never an option for me, I was still tormented hour after hour by the demons of worry, fear, and loneliness. A mind can wander into some deep pits of discouragement when there is nothing good to focus upon. I was still distant from God. A religious experience will never adequately replace the need for a relationship with God. I needed more than church; I needed God but I didn't know it. And if I did, I wouldn't know where to find Him. "Oh God, where are you now?"

Visiting room visits with family were very limited; a few minutes every other week, as you peered at each other through a thick glass barrier. It seemed no sooner did the visit begin, it was over, and I would be escorted back to my cell. Headaches and nausea would often accompany me after these visits. Back in my cell with nothing to do, I would try to sleep but sleep is never a permanent escape from reality. Sleep is not a problem eliminator. When you awake, the problem is still there.

Day after day, hour after hour, time would pass by so painfully slow. The caged mentality of jail life was beginning to overtake me. Sleep, eat, sleep, eat, sleep, eat.....you get the picture. There wasn't much else to do. Some of the other guys would chat with each other about absolutely nothing, just trash talk. I wasn't the least bit interested in anything but getting out. Everything was completely out of my control. No phone calls when I wanted, no going out with my friends, no getting in the car and driving to the nearest bar for a beer; seemingly everything was absolutely out of my control. I had taken a short nap one afternoon and when I awoke I saw something sitting on the bars of my cell. It was a book. Someone placed it there when I was sleeping. It wasn't a new book. The pages were torn and dog-eared, the binding was loose, and the cover stained from food and coffee. I picked it up and read the cover, "*The Way*". What kind of book was this? What was this book the way to?

I was facing the possibility of 20 years or more in prison. Fear and failure were my invisible cellmates. I don't remember hearing voices, but they were speaking to me. "You'll be here for a long time. What kind of future do you think you have now? Loser! Fool! Nobody can help you now!" Then I heard another voice. It also wasn't audible as much as it was an inner voice. It was a strong leading feeling, a prompting to pick up the book and read it. So I did. I opened "*The Way*" and started reading.

# *Could this be the Way?*

Page after page, I read for at least an hour. A tremendous peace came upon me as I read. My nervous system was tranquilized and I calmed down as I read. My eyes began to tire so I put the book down. I didn't understand all I was reading but I had peace when I read it. An hour or so would pass then fear and failure would begin speaking to me again. The peace that was so overwhelming when I read the book would fade away and I found myself back in reality. I picked the book up again and as I read it fear would leave and peace would replace it. I put the book down, fear returned and peace would leave. This scenario repeated itself each time I picked it up or put it down.

Several hours had passed and BAM it hit me. I was reading the Bible. Remember, although I was raised with plenty of religion, a Bible was not to be found in our home. Things have changed today but in the 1950's and 60's the Catholic Church discouraged Bible reading. We were told it was only for the priests and a select group of leaders. Thank God it's not like that today. I'm not sure why it took me so long to discover what I was reading. I should have looked at the cover a little closer. It read, "*The WAY*" (A modern translation Bible.) I don't know if I would have read it if I knew what it was. I'm not a big fan of thee, thou, cometh, leadeth, and restoreth. If "*The WAY*" had been written like that, I would not have "readeth it". Thank God for a variety of reliable Bible translations. The Bible became my daily source of comfort. I would read it for hours on end. The stories were coming alive and the peace of God that was beyond comprehension was capturing my heart.

As the week passed I continued to read. On the outside my attorney was making arrangements for my bail hearing. The result of the hearing was favorable. My bail was posted and in the early days of July 1975 I walked out of that jail. My parents posted a large sum of money as well as put their home up as bail-security in order for me to be released. Freedom has its price.

# *Twice Convicted*

Thirty days had passed since this ordeal all began, the longest thirty days of my life. I remember walking out of that jail and into my parents' car as we drove back to their home. I was 27 years old; a grown man, and like a child I was released into the custody of my parents. I was so grateful to be out, yet I knew that the road ahead of me would not be easy.

# Chapter Six

## Cross Conviction

*"...because our Gospel came to you not simply with words but with the Holy Spirit and deep conviction."*
*(1Thessalonians 1:5a)*

Living back at home wasn't easy. My parents didn't give me rules, regulations and curfews to follow yet I felt as though they had. It was actually my lawyer who laid down the rules. He continually reminded me how important it was to live as a model citizen as I awaited my day in court. I found out that it wasn't easy being good. I wanted to have a few beers and loosen up a little; I was told I better not. I wanted to tell my friends what happened that dreadful night; I was told to keep my mouth shut. I wanted to be myself; I was told not to. How in the world could I not be myself? I was told that I needed to change but I didn't know how to be different. The truth was I didn't think I needed to change. I still didn't get it. It should have been easy for me to recognize the seriousness of my faults but that false pride was keeping me from seeing who I really was.

Disregarding my attorney's sound advice I decided to have a few drinks at "*My Place*". I was embraced, encouraged, played some pool, and given free drinks. I had killed someone yet they treated me like I was a celebrity. "Bartender, I'll have another Budweiser." Forrest Gump described me best when he said, "Stupid is as stupid does." I didn't stay very long that night nor did I drink very much. I looked for my good friend Mike but he wasn't there. I always enjoyed his company. We'd always laughed together. I sure could have used a good laugh that night.

## *Twice Convicted*

"Where's Mike?" I asked the bartender. "Oh, we haven't seen him for a while. He doesn't come here anymore." "Why?" I asked. "What happened? Did he move?" One of the customers came over to me and said, "If you're looking for Mike why don't you try looking for him in church. He's got religion. His drinking days are over. His marriage has improved and he's back home with his wife, poor guy." It was time to go home so I finished my drink and left. As I was driving home all I could think about was Mike, not "Poor Guy," but "Lucky Guy." I had to talk with him. I wanted to hear more. I promised myself that I'd visit him first thing in the morning.

I had my morning coffee and headed out to Mike's. "Knock, knock." He came to the door and greeted me with a warm smile and a bear hug. He seemed so happy to see me. "Come on in. Maryellen and I were hoping you'd come by." She put on the coffee and we talked for a few hours. I wanted to know more about the change in his life and about the "religion" that he found. They were new converts, filled with zeal and enthusiasm. Their faces reflected a glow of joy, and their words seemed to penetrate deep within me. Our visit ended.......I drove home thinking, I want it. Whatever they had, I wanted it.

I decided to go back to church. I started attending Mass several times a week. It felt good when I was there, but when the service was over, I felt empty again. That's why I needed to go more than once a week. Sunday morning wasn't enough. I said my prayers but my prayers seemed to hit the glass ceiling and bounce back to me. I continued to visit Mike and Maryellen as often as I could. They would invite me over for dinner and we'd talk. I was getting frustrated because their joy was still evasive to me. I was doing everything I could think of. I was really working at it. I wasn't swearing as much, not drinking as much, and I was going to church multiple times each week.

Mike and Maryellen were new believers and they never thought about my need to have my own Bible. But they were my "Bible". God's love and peace was written all over them. When they talked about their faith it was as if God was speaking directly to me through them. I don't think they realized what a tremendous impact they had on my life.

They invited me to their home again for dinner. As we talked, I could see that they were concerned because of my lack of understanding. But my spiritual ignorance didn't stop them. I'm so glad they were patient with me. "It's good that you're going to church. It's great that your lifestyle is changing," they said, "but you need more than that; you need so much more. You need God in your heart." What did Mike mean when he said, "I need God in my heart?" He knew I was going to church!

The meal ended and it was time for me to leave. That's when Mike asked me the strangest question. "Phil, do you like to watch the *Tonight Show* starring Johnny Carson?" Why was he asking me that? Of course I liked watching it. I thought everyone liked Johnny Carson's late show. He was the King of late night. What kind of question was that? Then Mike said, "Phil, there's a program I want you to watch on TV. It's a talk show, a Christian talk show. If you like Carson, you'll like watching *The 700 Club*. Although it's not late night comedy it has a similar format. It's hosted by Pat Robertson, and he interviews a variety of guests. Do yourself a big favor; watch it."

It was July 19, 1975 11:00 pm and it was time to watch *The 700 Club*. My pride would keep me from telling anyone that I was watching a religious program. I was still too macho for that. My parents were camping for the weekend. I was alone. It was the perfect time to watch. I remember pulling down all the shades, turning off the lights, and locking the doors.

I was going to watch this program and no one was going to know about it. With the only light in the room coming from the TV set, I heard, "Welcome to *The 700 Club* with your host CBN President Pat Robertson, and his co-host Ben Kinchlow." Sitting back nervously on my recliner with my feet propped up I viewed the TV screen in the corner of the room. Within a few minutes I was being entertained by the conversation between Pat and Ben. They were good but they'd never replace Johnny Carson and his sidekick Ed McMahon.

Within a few minutes they introduced their guest for the show. I don't recall his name but I remember his story. He was a man whose life was once in shambles. He tried a variety of ways to get his life in order but time after time each new attempt failed to make a meaningful difference in his life. He'd even gone back to church. He sincerely wanted change but change wasn't happening. "That's me," I thought, "That's exactly how I feel." I was watching *The 700 Club* because I needed a change. Why was I watching another loser? His life wasn't any different than mine. We had both made a series of attempts to get it together but nothing worked. I was disappointed and about ready to turn off the TV. That's when Pat asked him the big question. "But your life was changed. How was your life changed?" I listened intently to his response. "I asked Jesus to come into my heart and my life hasn't been the same since."

I was rather disappointed by his answer. I thought he was going to say something more profound. I thought for sure he would have given me some direction, some hope, some advice. "I asked Jesus to come into my heart". Come on now! Let's get real. I'm a real man with a real problem; I need a real solution! I believe in God and all that but get serious; Jesus coming into my heart. First it was Santa then the Easter Bunny and the Tooth Fairy, and now it's Jesus coming into my heart. I've got a real problem. I'm not interested in hollow religious jargon.

I was about ready to get up from the chair and turn off the set when a phone number flashed across the screen. Call this number if you have questions or if you'd like to talk to one of our counselors. I sure would like to talk to someone. I was ready to give them a piece of my mind. Who do they think they are playing religious games with my mind? Someone should sue them. In anger I picked up the phone and dialed. I'm not sure what happened but my anger immediately subsided the moment someone answered the phone, "*700 Club,* may I help you?"

Within a few moments I was opening up my heart to a complete stranger in Virginia Beach, Virginia. I told her how my life was falling apart and how I was facing the possibility of many years in prison. She listened. She never condemned me nor did she approve of my actions. She just listened. She was genuinely concerned. She wanted to help. Her empathy could be discerned over the telephone. I could feel it. I didn't know what else to say, but she did. "Only Jesus can change things and turn your life around. You need Jesus in your heart." I heard those words before but this time they sounded like it was possible. Mike and Maryellen had planted the seeds of desire, now it was time for fruition.

"Let's pray; Repeat after me." HOLD ON! Wait a minute. I'm not ready for this. I'm not about to pray out loud with anyone let alone a stranger. I was ready to hang up when something strange happened. My imagination started kicking in and I saw the woman I was talking to in Virginia Beach. She was an elderly woman much like my grandmother who had passed away a few weeks earlier. She was doing her good deed by praying with people like me. How could I hang up on "Grandma"? I figured I'd go ahead and pacify her. I'll let her get a feather in her cap by praying for me; and when this phone call is over I'd never make another one like it again! Little did I realize that God had set before me a "Door of Hope" and I was about to enter.

# *Twice Convicted*

The prayer began. She prayed; I repeated after her. The prayer didn't last much longer than one minute. For the first 30 seconds or so the words I prayed seemed empty to me. At one point I almost hung up on her. All I was doing was repeating her words. Then it hit me, **my first conviction**. I was convicted of my sin. *"When he comes, [the Holy Spirit] He will convict the world of guilt in regard to sin and righteousness and judgment." (John 16:8)* I actually believed what I was praying and the words were sincerely coming from my heart. I was indeed a guilty sinner and I needed God's forgiveness and a change in my life. I'm so glad I didn't hang up.

We finished praying and she congratulated me for becoming a child of God. I'd made a lot of bad choices in my life. I tried to change my ways but all my attempts failed miserably. I'd finally made the right choice. I'd found the "agent of change". His name is Jesus. She asked me how I felt. I told her that I felt OK, but nothing phenomenal. She reminded me that although feelings are valuable my experience was validated by the sincerity of my heart not by any particular feelings or lack of them. She asked for my name and address so they could send me material that would help me in my new birth. She reminded me that my name was written down in heaven and God's plan for my life would be fulfilled if I followed after Him. She said goodbye. I said the same.......and we hung up. It was July 19, 1975 11:30 pm. I'd surrendered my life to God and I was "Born-Again".

The next few hours were to be surreal. After hanging up the phone I simply sat there in my recliner. The TV was still on but I was no longer paying attention to it. There was something going on inside of me that I had never experienced before. As I share with you what happened, keep in mind I cannot fully explain it, all I can do is tell you the facts as I remember them. Whether it was physical or spiritual, I'm not totally sure. I believe it was a combination of both.

As I sat there I suddenly felt an unusual presence filling the room and filling me. It was extremely peaceful yet strange. I have since come to discern this as the presence of God, but that night I didn't have any idea what was happening. I felt light, as if something heavy had been lifted off my shoulders. I felt alive like never before. I also felt fearful. What was happening to me? This feeling was totally overwhelming. I wanted it to go; I wanted it to remain. I was enjoying the moment; I thought I was losing my mind. Then it happened. It seemed as if the recliner was slightly hovering over the living room carpet. It wasn't moving around the room, just hovering in the same area. Was this actually happening or was it my imagination? (Please don't disregard what I'm saying just because it doesn't make sense. It wasn't making any sense to me either.) "What's happening here? I've got to get off this chair!" I wasn't sure but I believed it had something to do with that prayer I said. Or maybe I was losing it; after all, I did have a lot going on in my life. I tried to make sense of the moment but to no avail. The chair was hovering and that was that. I wasn't enjoying this ride. I had to get off the chair; I had to get my feet on solid ground. I gingerly removed myself from my "hovercraft" and planted my feet firmly on the carpet.

Guess what? The hovering continued. It wasn't the chair after all. Now I was hovering. Again, whether this was happening in the natural or spiritual realm I wasn't absolutely sure, all I knew was it happened. A few minutes had passed since it all began. I was enjoying it. I cautiously began walking as if I was gliding on ice or moon-walking.

"What in the world (or heaven) is going on?" I never felt anything remotely close to it. It was every enjoyable amusement ride thrill rolled up into one. This was no hallucinating event nor was it my imagination playing games with me; this was happening. This hovering continued for the next hour or so. When I sat down, the chair hovered. When I got up, I hovered. I didn't have any answers to what was happening; all I knew was a peaceful presence had captured me and I was totally engulfed in it. I can fully understand reader skepticism at this point, but I share here honestly my experiences of that night.

I tried calling Mike and Maryellen; I had a plethora of questions to ask them. No answer. By now it was well after midnight and they were probably in bed. The feeling wasn't subsiding but I was beginning to tire. I was mentally exhausted yet refreshed. I wanted this moment to last forever but it wasn't going to. I finally calmed down enough to hover myself into bed. With mind swirling with questions I drifted off to sleep. The next thing I knew it was morning. I got up from bed. No hovering sensation. It was over. But I felt different. The burden was lifted and great peace was upon me. Within a few days I was at Mike's house. I told him about my *700 Club* experience and that I had asked the Lord to come into my heart. I didn't tell him about my hovercraft chair and my moon-walking. It was several years before I was bold enough to share that experience with anyone. I was still dealing with huge amounts of pride and I didn't want anyone to think I was crazy, especially with my pending court case. We got into Mike's car and drove to Bender's Christian Bookstore in Williamsville, New York (north of Buffalo). He bought me my first Bible. There was so much for me to discover about my new found faith and I was indeed eager to learn.

# Chapter Seven

## Charismatic Encounter

*"Do not conform any longer to the pattern of this world, but be transformed by the renewing of your mind."*
*(Romans 12:2)*

It would be approximately nine months before my trial began. Nine months of waiting to see what the future held for me. Nine months of limbo for an impatient man. Although nine months isn't necessarily long, it's long enough for seasons to change, for barren fields to produce a harvest, and it's long enough for conception to give way to birth. It was nine months for this new born Christian to drink in the milk of God's Word. The garden of my life needed serious attention. If my life was going to change I had to surrender into the hands of the Master Gardener. There was (still is) a lot of work to do in my life. Impossible with man but with God all things are possible. Although God knew me before my birth, His plan for my life was only beginning to be understood by me. *"Before I formed you in the womb I knew you, before you were born I set you apart; I appointed you as a prophet to the nations."* (*Jeremiah 1:5*) Those nine months were challenging and tumultuous as I was being changed from the inside out.

Surrender wasn't coming easy for me. I dug my heels in. I was defiant and resistant. A rebellious and prideful personality like mine wasn't going to give up easily. There were enormous amounts of clutter from my sinful nature that had to come out. Yet God was working in me removing the trash and making room for something better; His fruit.

Little by little this change was taking place. At times I was in the midst of a Dr. Jekyll and Mr. Hyde experience giving the appearance of hypocrisy. It wasn't hypocrisy; I was being changed. One day I was in church, the next at the bar. Praising God today, using obscenities tomorrow. When you are in the midst of the metamorphic stage it's seldom understood and never without pain. It's always chaotic and your daily actions are rather unpredictable. The old nature is reluctant to die. It doesn't want to make way for the new. If you are struggling through this stage in your life, don't give up. The rewards for enduring are worth the fight.

As change was taking place in my life there was also change happening in the Catholic Church and it was affecting multitudes of people all across the world. It's been estimated that over 230 countries and millions of people were impacted by this movement that began in the early 1970's often referred to as the "Catholic Charismatic Renewal". God's spirit was moving mightily within the church. Healings and miracles were taking place. Believers were being filled with the Holy Spirit leaving them with a deep hunger to know more about the Bible. The public praise and worship of God was taken out of the closet and shouted from the rooftops. St. Catherine's Roman Catholic Church in West Seneca, NY was one of those places where God's Spirit was being poured out and touching many lives. Even though I was going to Mass each week, I was still hungry for more. I wanted a deeper experience with God. As I read my Bible every day, the desire to know more about God increased.

The church was only a few miles from home so I decided to attend. I was a little late and the parking lot was packed. What's going on here? I must have the wrong night. With all these cars, it must be BINGO Night. So many people wouldn't be at a prayer meeting. I was expecting a handful at best. I was ready to turn my car around and head home when I noticed people carrying what looked like Bibles. I didn't know what to expect, but I was going in. I'd sit in the back pew just in case I had to make a getaway. Nervously I walked into the building and into the sanctuary. It was empty. What's going on in here? Where is everyone? I saw someone and asked him where the prayer meeting was. "Downstairs" he said. "That's where all the action is." Action! What kind of action do you find in church?

I walked down the stairs to the lower level and as I opened the door of the fellowship hall I was not ready for what I saw. Hundreds of men, women, and even children sitting in a huge circle with their hands lifted up and loudly singing praises to the Lord. They wore huge smiles as they sang and their faces were radiant. I stood in the background. There were no pews in this room, only folding chairs. Many were standing for it appeared they had run out of chairs. I peered through the large group of people so I could see inside the circle. I saw a couple people with guitars, a few microphones, and a song leader. There wasn't any overhead projector for the words but the lyrics were simple enough to learn rather quickly. There were a few lyric handouts but clearly not enough to accommodate everyone there.

We sang for about an hour with prayers woven throughout the chorus. These were different kinds of prayers, not what I was used to. Not memorized prayers but words that seemed to flow from the hearts of those who prayed. They were actually talking to God and they knew it. I didn't understand all that was going on but I knew it was right. Eventually the prayers and singing stopped as Father Len opened his Bible and taught the lesson for the night.

Father Len was different from most Catholic priests in the 70's. He was hugely charismatic with the joy of the Lord being his greatest asset. He spoke confidently and with authority. His voice captured those in attendance as he unfolded the Scriptures revealing the mysteries hidden within. He ended with prayer and the singing started again.

At about 9 o'clock the service ended and people began to slowly leave. There wasn't a mad rush for the parking lot. Many lingered and chatted with each other. Small groups spontaneously formed as people prayed for each other until a custodian flicked the lights on and off signaling us that it was time to leave. I went back to my car and drove home. That night I knew I had been in the presence of the Lord. What I experienced was something that deeply satisfied. Not only was I in a room filled with hundreds of people who genuinely communicated with God; I talked to Him too, and I knew he heard me. God was working in my life and changes were taking place.

# Chapter Eight

## Court Conviction

*"The Lord is slow to anger but great in power;*
*The Lord will not leave the guilty unpunished."*
*(Nahum 1:3a)*

The seasons passed, the year ended, and 1976 finally arrived. It would soon be time for my day in court. By February of that year the proceedings began. There were preliminary hearings, court dates to be arranged, and pre-trial motions. Unless you had been through it you wouldn't know how involved it would be. I had countless sessions with my attorney as we prepared my defense. The prosecution was busily preparing its case against me. My attorney and the prosecution met several times in the judge's chambers to privately discuss my court date. An agreement was made and my trial began mid March of 1976. It was time for us to get busy. The first step was the all-important jury selection. It wasn't easy. It took over two weeks to agree upon the selections. With that task behind us it was time for the trial to begin. For the next 4 weeks I would be facing them, the jury of my peers. Next on the agenda were opening statements made by the defense and the prosecution. I was facing a charge of 2$^{nd}$ degree murder and if convicted could face incarceration of 20 years or more in a New York State prison. The trial went as expected. The District Attorney subpoenaed witnesses who testified against me. He did his best to portray me as a cold-blooded murderer. My attorney presented a number of mitigating circumstances in the hope of persuading the jury to render a verdict of not guilty.

# *Twice Convicted*

Closing arguments were made and the jury was escorted to the deliberation room. My fate was now in the hands of the jury. We left the court room and waited in the hall. A few hours passed when the court clerk notified us the jury had a verdict. We hurriedly entered back into the court room as the judge and jury took their seats. I nervously stood before the judge and the jury. There was silence in the room as the judge read the verdict. "The jury finds the defendant Philip J. Cebula guilty of 2nd Degree Manslaughter." This was my **Second Conviction;** my first conviction was the conviction of my sin.

The judge continued my bail and I went home to spend the next few weeks preparing for my inevitable incarceration. Approximately 2 weeks later I returned to the court room for my formal sentencing. "This court sentences you to a maximum of 10 years in a New York State Correctional Facility." The gavel came down as my family wept. I was handcuffed and escorted out of the courtroom and back to the cell where I would spend my last night before being transferred to Attica.

Early the next morning those of us who were recently convicted were escorted from our cells to our waiting bus. Wearing handcuffs and foot shackles we shuffled on board. "Find a comfortable seat", the corrections officer said as we headed down the highway to our destination of Attica, New York. This wasn't my first trip to the Attica region, a quaint community in western New York known for its beauty. To local residents it was a place to enjoy fishing and camping surrounded in a country-like atmosphere. It was also known as a residence for the most hardened criminals. It was ATTICA PRISON to which I was headed. I may have looked calm and confident on the outside but inwardly I was afraid. Sometimes fear has a way of masquerading in false courage.

# *Court Conviction*

It seemed like a long 30-mile trip from the county jail to Attica Prison. Included on the bus were seasoned convicts as well as first timers like me. There wasn't much conversation that day as most of us looked out the windows as if we were saying goodbye to Buffalo and everything outside the bus. About 10 miles into our journey, Larry, one of the guys sitting next to me, motioned that he had something in his hand to give me. He was strange, the kind of guy that was in and out of prison all his life and always blamed others for his problems. I am not normally inclined to label people as losers, but if I had been compelled to characterize him, Larry would have received such a label. He was a constant complainer and thought the whole world was out to get him. If you said up, he said down; if you said right, Larry said left. Nothing seemed to agree with him. Little did I know that eventually Larry would be housed down the hall from me in B-Block.

He hated the cops and despised the screws (corrections officers). At the time Larry was about 60 years old, but his actions and demeanor were that of a 25 year old juvenile delinquent. He seemed to live in a constant state of trouble and wanted to pull you into his world. "Pssst", he said, "Open your hand." I wasn't sure what he wanted but I acknowledged his request and opened my hand. Very discreetly he placed a little red pill into the palm of my hand. Apparently he had smuggled this contraband onto the bus. "Take this," he said rather quietly, "you'll feel better when we get to the wall." I didn't have to ask him what it was. I knew it would get me high. I wasn't sure what I was going to do. I had a decision to make; and I was running out of time to make it. Fear and trepidation of what was possibly awaiting me behind the walls of Attica were waging war on the battle field of my mind. I may have appeared to look calm, but I wasn't.

# *Twice Convicted*

Living the life of a Born-Again Christian was rather easy when I was out on bail but now I'm going to prison. Does Christianity work behind the walls? Could faith in God keep me safe at Attica? Would God watch over me like the Bible says? I held on tightly to that little red pill squeezing it until the palm of my hand turned red from the food coloring. I looked at Larry and said, "Thanks man, I sure could use it." Part of me wanted to be one of the guys and part wanted to be one of God's men. But my biggest concern was the fear of the unknown and I considered briefly escaping from the reality of prison life by ingesting this pill. What should I do? I decided to pretend that I put it in my mouth as my "drug dealer" watched me with pleasure. "You'll be OK now." he said, "We'll be at the wall pretty soon." But the pill was still in my hand. There was still enough time to take it or inconspicuously let it drop to the floor of the bus. Before my sentencing I was so very sure that I was going to walk the walk of faith. I knew of the joy and comfort that only God could produce in one's life. I knew what would be the right thing to do but I was still having trouble doing it. My spirit was indeed willing but my flesh was weak.

As I pondered my decision I looked up and there it was, the WALL. I'm told the wall is forty feet high but to me it looked one hundred and forty feet. I looked at the pill in my hand as I glanced at the imposing wall before me. My time was up. It was decision time. The handwriting was on the WALL. I opened my hand and let the pill fall to the floor. We arrived at the WALL. The bus rolled to a stop and the door opened.

Still wearing our handcuffs and shackles, we shuffled to the front gate. It opened and I entered it. I knew I'd made the right decision. The comforting presence of God was strong on me and I knew everything was going to be alright. My decision was final. There would be no turning back. That day, at the age of 28, I walked into Attica State Prison and became a FREE MAN! *"So if the Son sets you free, you will be free indeed."* (John 8:36)

# Chapter Nine

## Home Away from Home

*"He blesses the home of the righteous."*
*(Proverbs 3:33b)*

I entered Attica in May 1976, almost 5 years after the infamous event known as the Attica Prison Riots had taken place. It was estimated over 1,000 of the 2,200 inmates had taken part in this four-day bloody confrontation which ended when New York State Governor Nelson Rockefeller ordered an assault to retake the prison. Tear gas was dropped by helicopters as state troopers armed with rifles entered the facility. The assault was fast and furious; 39 people had lost their lives. The death toll would include 10 correctional officers and civilian employees. Of the 29 prisoners killed 4 would be vigilante killings. Many others had been seriously wounded inside these walls. The tension still lingered like a rancid corpse decaying in some forgotten hallway. The battle scars still remained; heavily leaving an atmosphere you could almost cut with a knife. The smoke was gone but not the pain. The debris was picked up but not the fear that remained. The state troopers and their helicopters were gone but the walls of the court-yard were etched from the bullets that pelted them. With the front gates closed securely behind me I began my "time" in this prison environment. My first few hours involved prisoner intake and classification. Mug shots, finger prints, and all the necessary routine procedures had to be performed. I was even given a new identification, 76C312, and a new address, Attica, New York.

I was then escorted to my cell by way of "Times Square". No more handcuffs and shackles. Where could I go? There were approximately 12 prison gates that clanged shut behind before I arrived deep within the prison at "Times Square". I always wanted to visit Times Square but not this one. This undoubtedly is the most secure place in Attica Prison. It's a place in the center of the prison where four corridors meet, much like an intersection with each hall leading to one of the prison's major sections (blocks).

I was taken to my new home in B-Block cell #13. This would be my home for a while. It didn't take very long to realize life in prison is routine; wake up, breakfast, work assignment, lunch, back to work, supper, some free time, and lights out. We were always being counted (day and night) in hope of preventing anyone from escaping. Only one person has ever escaped from Attica, Joe "*Mad Dog*" Sullivan in 1971, only to be apprehended two months later and brought back to prison. I didn't have any plans of escaping my "friendly confines" yet I was determined not to let prison routine become my way of doing time. Far too many inmates are trapped by the routines while forfeiting their opportunity to discover purpose in life. I wasn't going to wait until I was released from prison to be used by God.

As most prisons are, Attica is a city unto itself. Isolated behind its walls are the daily routines that go un-noticed by those on the outside. Much of society has a "lock them up and throw away the key" mentality. Men and women die every day yet no obituaries are found in local newspapers. Complaints of prisoner brutality are often ignored. Unless a full blown riot breaks out very little is worthy enough to make national (or even local) news. Educational programs are offered but illiteracy remains high.

Relatively few take advantage of these programs. Others do and achieve college degrees but usually without the blessing of having friends and family with them to celebrate their achievement.

Birthdays come and go without parties, presents and cake. It's a lonely forgotten place. Suicides are common especially during the holidays. Many have severe emotional problems and should be in mental health units but because of overcrowded state hospitals they find themselves in maximum security prisons not getting the proper care they need. Many of these men do not have anyone to advocate on their behalf resulting in their continual decline of mental health. Few receive visits with regularity. Some never do. At night when the lights go out grown men can be heard crying yet no one listens or seems to care. Perhaps many of you are thinking, "Hey, it's prison. It's not supposed to be a picnic. Crimes have been committed and a price must be paid. Suck it up!"

Don't misunderstand what I'm saying. I don't think a prison is called to be a palace. There are a few "country club" prison facilities across this nation but the typical prison is indeed a prison. The average size of your four grey walled prison home is 6'x8'. Included in your estate is a bed, sink, toilet, a small desk with built in cabinet, and one low watt ceiling light. Over time an inmate might accumulate a few more items but this is your typical unit. If you thought we all had color TV's, computers and phones you've been watching too many movies. Prisoners are not treated like celebrities. We are criminals and were treated as such. Few of the estimated two million incarcerated in the United States on any given day are candidates for "Man of the Year." Some are in adamant denial, refusing to waver in their claim of innocence. There are those who may be wrongly convicted yet most of us knew why we were there.

# *Twice Convicted*

We were more than criminals; we were convicted criminals. It's not surprising that much of society has turned their backs on us.

Rehabilitation is not working. The rate of recidivism is out of control. Approximately 95% are eventually released back into society not equipped to lead productive, lives with their average 7th grade level education. Within three years of release almost 70% are re-arrested and over 50% are re-incarcerated resulting in extreme prison overcrowding. The departments of parole and probation cannot adequately supervise the number of people assigned to them. The "correctional" system is not correcting the problem and no one seems to have an answer. Many of America's prisoners are forgotten people, out of sight and out of mind. But according to the Bible prisoners are not a throw-away society. We have a mandate from God that reads, "*Continue to remember those in prison as if you were together with them in prison.*" (Hebrews 13:3) Jesus said that he came to "*proclaim freedom for the prisoners*". (Luke 4:18) We would soon find out that Attica was on His list! Attica, it's your turn. The country watched the Attica riot bring death and destruction. Now it was time to witness a revival that would usher in abundant life. History records a number of great revivals but very little has been said about the Revival in Attica.

# Chapter Ten

## Small Beginnings

*"Who despises the day of small things?"*
*(Zechariah 4:10a)*

My first encounter with a group of Christians in Attica was at the Friday Night Bible Study. That's the night when Christian believers gathered together for a time of fellowship and to hear the Word of God. With my Gideon's Pocket New Testament in hand, I was escorted to the Bible study. My expectations were high that night. I imagined walking into a large room crowded with men hungry for God to speak to them. Much to my surprise the room was very small and so was our "church" which totaled seven inmates including myself. Not much of a church. I was rather disappointed seeing such a small group for I was anticipating the room being filled to capacity. Were we the only ones who wanted God to help us? Were we the only ones who knew God could help us? Were we the entire Church in Attica? Twenty-two hundred men behind the walls yet only seven came to hear the Word of God. Something about it didn't seem right.

But that didn't stop us from entering into the presence of God. Clark, our inmate piano player, couldn't read a note of music but he sure could play that thing. He sat there and turned those old songs into honky-tonk hymns. He didn't just tickle the ivories. He hammered the keys. When he played the room came alive as we opened up our hymnals and began to sing. The old hymns erupted with excitement as our voices harmonized praises to our God. Hymn after hymn we sang without interruption. Eventually our small room was transformed into the chamber of God's presence as a few extemporaneous prayers were spoken. This was a new experience for me. I seldom heard anyone praying impromptu. At first I thought it might be sacrilegious, but I soon realized these prayers were genuine and flowing from the hearts of believers to the heart of God. Soon I was doing the same. Jesus said "*Where two or three gather in my name, there I am with them." (Matthew 18:20)* We met the criteria. We had seven, and God was faithful to meet us there.

Eventually Clark closed his piano and our volunteer chaplain, Rev. Normand Farrington began his Bible study. Week after week Pastor Farrington would remind us of God's love. He would not end the service without quoting *"Cast all your care upon Him; for He cares for you." (1st Peter 5:7)* We had a number of community volunteers who rotated coming in on Friday nights, all of whom were loved and appreciated by us. Among them were Rev. Rob Wright and Rev. Jeff Carter. Eventually, they both became state hired chaplains. They all greatly impacted my life.

Sundays were not much different. Although a few more men responded to the Sunday service it was still rather sparse with 25-30 men meeting in a huge auditorium that would not have any problem accommodating several hundred men. On movie nights the auditorium would be filled to capacity but on Sundays the church barely filled the first few rows.

One might easily think that our church in Attica Prison was insignificant. Yes, we were a small group, but we were not insignificant. Our chaplains taught us well; that we had purpose and were called to be the salt of the earth and the light of the world in which we lived. I remember saying to Pastor Farrington, "When I get out, I'm going to make a difference in the world." He looked squarely into my eyes and said "Why wait to make a difference? Do it now!" His words pierced me like a knife. I knew I shouldn't keep my experience a secret. The church is never called to do that. Other men needed to hear about the life changing power of the Gospel.

I didn't have a lot of experience at evangelism and my knowledge of Scripture was still very limited. Yet there were two things I did have to share; my story and my peace of mind. Our testimony is one of the most powerful evangelistic tools we have. We don't have to be theologians or eloquent speakers to share our experience. The gift is not the messenger, it's the message. All you need is your story, the story of how Jesus Christ changed your life. The peace of God upon your life during difficult times will also persuade others to listen to your story. As believers in Christ we have a clear mandate from scripture saying, *"We are therefore Christ's ambassadors, as though God were making His appeal through us.........." (2Corinthians 5:20)* The big question was; would I be His ambassador in Attica Prison? I knew what the answer was. Revival was a long way off but you've got to begin somewhere, one person at a time. *"Who despises the day of small things? (Zechariah 4:10a)* I was a man on the cusp of his mission to set the captives free.

# Chapter Eleven

## Big Jim and Old Sparky

*"My relatives have gone away;*
*my closest friends have forgotten me"*
*(Job 19:14)*

If only these walls could talk. There are many prison stories that will never be told because much of what has taken place behind prison bars remains locked within its walls. The popular axiom "What happens in Vegas stays in Vegas," would accurately apply to prison life. Only a few prison accounts will ever break out to reach the streets for others to hear. Most men and women are reluctant to tell others about their prison experiences. We are not proud of our incarceration. Any former inmate who has ever filled out an application for employment knows of the struggle he or she has when asked the question, "Have you ever been convicted of a felony?" I have chosen to open up my closet and share these stories. God has done wonderful things for me, and I have witnessed much while incarcerated. It is my prayer that God will be glorified as I share these prison accounts with you.

One such story is the story of "Big Jim". All it took was one look from him and you knew he was a hardened criminal. Standing about 6'6" and weighing 250 lbs, he could have been mistaken for a professional football linebacker. His face had a small but noticeable scar on the left cheek giving him the appearance of a deeply angry man. His voice was gruff and raspy, and his eyes dark and dagger like. One never knew what "big Jim" was capable of doing. Few ever entered into conversation with Jim. He was a loner. He never smiled, he seldom spoke, and he instilled fear in those around him. He looked like he was ready to snap at any moment, and the best thing anyone could do was keep their distance from him. He was a lifer with no possibility of parole.

Although no one had the courage to ask him, the word in "B" Block was that Jim and his older brother were responsible for the murder of a New York State trooper in the late 60's. He was sentenced to die in the electric chair at Sing-Sing Maximum Security Prison in Ossining, New York. The last execution in New York was when Eddie Mays sat in the electric chair in 1963. While Jim waited his turn to be strapped into "Old Sparky" (as the inmates would refer to the infamous chair) the United States Supreme Court suspended the death penalty and declared it unconstitutional. Jim was taken off death row and eventually transferred to Attica Prison. Capital punishment remained suspended from 1972 through 1976. Since then each state has the right to determine its own ruling concerning the death penalty. At the time of this writing, New York State still does not have the death penalty.

**Old Sparky**

One day as I walked past "Big Jim" our eyes caught and he said "Hi". It wasn't his usual harsh gruff voice but rather a much softer gentle tone that seemed to be in search of something. His eyes were not cold as ice and his facial features were relaxed and friendly. I responded back, "Hi Big Jim", as I continued on my way wondering why he had initiated the greeting. Little did I know but this brief encounter would eventually lead to a big change in his life. Day after day that simple exchange would take place. ("Hi Phil........Hi Big Jim") After a while Jim would go out of his way just to say "Hi" and the smile on his face was increasing each time. Jim needed a friend and God was going to use me to meet that need in his life. Jim's friends and family had long ago abandoned him. Like so many prisoners, Big Jim never received visits nor did he ever receive any mail. *"My relatives have gone away; my closest friends have forgotten me" (Job 19:14)* "Alone" in Attica Prison is a terrible place to be.

I was still being cautious around him. I wasn't sure about him. Could I trust him? Should I trust him? One thing I learned while incarcerated is that many inmates resent the fact that others are happy. If they are miserable, you should be miserable too. As I was experiencing the "joy of the Lord" did Jim resent it or was he attracted to it?

There are a few perks in prison, one of them being the commissary. If you had a few dollars in your inmate account, once every other week you would be escorted to the "store" to treat yourself to some candy or some little treat. Commissary items included pens, paper, stamps, candy, shaving cream, canned foods, cigarettes, soda, and ice cream. Because we didn't have refrigerators the half-gallons of ice cream had to be eaten right away. I think I can still polish off a half gallon in one sitting. On hot summer days you would often buy your friends ice cream and when it was their turn to go to the commissary they in turn would do the same. So each time I went I usually bought four half gallons (one for Carlos, Mike, David and myself). Ice cream in Attica was always considered a special treat.

One day I purchased five half gallons and as I went back to my cell I stopped in front of Big Jim's and gave him the extra one I'd purchased. "Here you go Jim. I thought you'd enjoy some ice cream. Hurry up and eat it before it melts." Jim just nodded, not a word spoken. I actually thought that Jim didn't know how to say "thank you" but I knew he appreciated the gift. Locked up when the temperature is 90 degrees outside it's much hotter on the inside. You didn't think we had AC did you?

Afternoon yard activity ended and I was escorted back to my cell. As I walked past Jim's "house" he nodded and said his usual "Hi" but this time he seemed to have a little smirk on his face. I didn't think much about it until I walked into my cell and found something placed in my bed. It was a beautiful glass painting of Jesus praying in the Garden of Gethsemane. Glass painting is popular with inmates. It helps pass the time away. These paintings were often sold to visitors. (It's one of the few ways to make a couple extra dollars.) Some of these beautiful paintings would sell for as much as $100-$200. The one placed on my bed could have easily been sold for $200 or more. What added to its value was the very fact that it was painted by an Attica inmate. "How do you like it?" I heard Jim shout down the corridor. I knew it was a work of his hands. He spent much of his time painting and he was very talented in his craft. I had a beauty. Was he showing it to me so I could sell it for him in the visiting room? Remember, Jim didn't receive visits so he wouldn't have any venue to sell these paintings. I shouted back to him, "Great work Jim. You've got yourself quite a talent." Even if it had been a terrible painting I surely would not have had the guts to tell him. I went to bed that night wondering what was up with the painting.

# Big Jim and Old Sparky

Occasionally when the recreation yard was closed because weather was unfavorable our cells would be opened and we could freely walk up and down our corridors and spend time with other inmates. I was sitting in my cell reading my Bible and a shadow blocked the light from the hallway. I looked up and standing in front of my cell was Jim. This was highly unusual for him. He spent almost all of his time to himself. "So you like the glass painting huh"? Again I told him it was really great work. "What would you like me to do with it?" I asked. "It's for you", he replied, "It's a gift for buying me that ice cream. Thank you." I could tell he was not comfortable saying those two words (thank you). He went on to say that in his forty plus years of life he never remembered receiving a gift from anyone. He was clearly choked up as he continued to tell me how much that ice cream meant to him. He couldn't understand why anyone would do such a thing. I told him it was nothing. He didn't owe me anything but he insisted that I receive the glass painting as his "thank you gift".

The time was right for me to begin telling him about the love of God. I proceeded to share the gospel story with him. While sitting on the edge of my bed he listened intently for about 30 minutes. It was soon time for him to leave and go back to his cell. I asked him if he'd like to invite Jesus into his heart and when I said that he backed away and quickly changed the tone of his voice. "No, I'm not ready for that. You can read your Bible and all that stuff, but that's not for me." As he left I told him God had a plan for his life even though he was a lifer in Attica prison and that I would be praying for him. "You do that", he said rather sarcastically. I remembered hearing the phrase, *"Don't tell me I've got a friend in Jesus, without showing me first that I've got a friend in you."* and I decided to make "Big Jim" my friend. It wasn't going to be an easy task, but I was determined to do it.

I started to look for opportunities to chat with him. Sometimes he welcomed conversation, other times not. I realized that if I was going to befriend him I had to be willing to change some of my daily routine. I had to make him a part of my everyday agenda. I worked in the prison metal shop and so did Jim. This made it relatively easy to talk with him on a daily basis. My invitations to join us for Bible studies and church services were continually declined. His reply was always the same, "I told you, I'm not ready for that stuff!" But I could see the day he would come. I could see the day Jim would open his heart to Jesus. By faith I saw it before it happened. *"Now faith is the substance of things hoped for; the evidence of things not seen." (Hebrews 11:1*) Little by little I was earning the right to tell Jim about Jesus.

One day we were sitting together in my cell and the time came. His heart was ready for the change. We talked a little about his past and about God's future for him. *"For I know the plans I have for you," declares the LORD, "plans to prosper you and not to harm you, plans to give you hope and a future." (Jeremiah 29:11*) I looked at him and said, "I believe God spared you the electric chair and He is now offering you His mercy seat. Are you ready? "In a soft voice and with a small tear in his eye, Jim responded, "I'm ready". Right there in B-block cell #13 Jim became a new man. He looked the same, the scar was still there and his voice still rather gruff, but he was a new man. Standing 6'6" and weighing 250 lbs, a new babe in Christ. Jim eventually transferred out of B-block, but I continued seeing him in church and Bible studies with a smile on his face and a Bible in his hand. Jim was now my friend and my brother.

# Chapter Twelve

## Prison Snitch

*"You are my hiding place; you will protect me from trouble and surround me with songs of deliverance."*
*(Psalm 32:7)*

We were in the middle of a heat wave with temperatures reaching well into the 90's all week long. It was hot and tempers flared even hotter. We couldn't take the day off and "escape" to the beach, and again I remind you, we did not have AC to make things cooler. When it's hot in Attica there's very little you can do about it. Many had work assignments in which they perspired regardless of the temperature outside. Yet when it was hot outside it was that much hotter at work. Several inmates were taken to the prison infirmary with heat exhaustion, while others suffered cramps and severe dehydration. Some spoke out and complained about conditions but the system has very little empathy for such complaint. No one wanted another uprising but an inmate strike was a strong possibility. Word was secretively spreading through the prison grapevine that prisoners were going to stage a lock-in strike, a condition in which inmates will refuse to go to their work assignment and remain in their cells. The prison system considers this a very serious offense that would result in disciplinary actions. This was to occur on Monday morning. (The prison grapevine could move information faster than the internet) There would be penalties for those who participated, especially for the organizers. My eyes have witnessed brutality on inmates by some corrections officers; it's not a pleasant thing to watch. I'm also aware of the consequences wrought by some inmates upon other inmates who didn't go along with the majority. It can be a dilemma with serious consequence; leaving no simple remedy.

Friday afternoon finally arrived. Most work assignments were now off for the weekend. What would the next two days produce? Would the prevailing tension be calmed, or would an undercurrent of momentum give strength to the plans of its organizers? Were things quiet or brewing? No one was talking openly but the grapevine was on overload. It was an eerie weekend. Was this the calm before the storm? Saturday came and went without any fanfare. Weekends in Attica often meant visits from family. The visiting rooms were usually overcrowded and oftentimes your visitors had to leave early in order to make room for others. If you didn't have a visit you probably spent much of your weekend hand-washing your personal clothing, writing letters, in the recreation yard, or quite simply, doing nothing. Boredom prevails for many. I reiterate, many inmates never get visits or seldom receive mail.

Sunday is a day of worship for many in Attica. It's when the prison visiting room is usually filled to capacity and it's when the recreation yard is crowded with inmates trying to keep busy doing nothing. I would often have a visit on Sunday afternoon but that Sunday I was not expecting one. I had three options. Stay in my cell until supper, go outside into the overcrowded recreation yard or attend the Hispanic Worship Service. I decided to attend the service. Although most of the inmates that attended were Hispanic there were always a few that were not. Because of this it was usually interpreted into English so I would occasionally find myself attending. I always enjoyed these services. The music was alive and filled with expression and excitement. It seemed as if each time I went the sermon message was exactly what I needed to hear.......but not this day. This day would be different. The music portion of the service finished and it was now time for the sermon. Most weeks there were volunteers from the region that would come in and lead the service.

Occasionally, when volunteers could not make it, one of the inmates would lead the service. An announcement was made that this would be one of those Sundays. The Spirit of God was mighty that day as we praised God with loud voices and a wide variety of musical instruments such as drums, guitars, keyboard, maracas, guiro's, tambourines, congas and other traditionally Hispanic instruments. An inmate stood behind the pulpit and announced he would be our "guest" speaker for the day and the service would not be interpreted that day. That was OK with me. The Spirit of God speaks in many languages and I was being ministered to by the atmosphere of praise and the presence of God that filled the auditorium that afternoon. Sitting next to me was my very good friend Carlos, who assured me that he would interpret personally for me if I wanted him to. "Thanks Carlos, I'll let you know if I need your help."

The first few minutes of his message seemed right. Men shouted back "Amen" and "Gloria a Dios" as he stood there reading from the Bible. Suddenly the expression on his face changed. His countenance of joy was instantly replaced by a weightier matter. The room became quiet as the shouts of praise were soon reduced to whispers of serious concern. The longer I sat there the more my inner man was becoming troubled. I discerned a big change in the spiritual atmosphere. Heaviness soon filled the room. The presence of the Lord vacated the auditorium as a dark cloud of concern and suspicion rapidly replaced it. I didn't have to speak the language to understand that something was not right. I leaned over to Carlos and asked him what was going on. He signaled me to be quiet. After a few minutes I leaned over again and said, "What's going on?" Carlos then leaned over and whispered in my ear, "We're planning an inmate strike. Now be quiet before we get into trouble." I looked at him and said, "Are you kidding me? I'm out of here. I don't want anything to do with this. I'm leaving."

This was easier said than done. In prison an inmate just doesn't get up and leave whenever he wants. I made a choice to be there and there I would stay. Exceptions were seldom made. I needed one of those exceptions that day as I walked to the back of the room and asked the corrections officer (C.O.) if I could go back to my cell. He looked at me and reminded me of the policies. "Do you think you're special?" I didn't respond to that question but inwardly I said, "Yes I am. I am a child of God and I have His favor on my life." He then asked me why I wanted to leave. I surely didn't want to tell him the real reason so I said, "The service isn't being interpreted. I don't speak Spanish." He smiled and said "You should have thought of that before you came." He chuckled and said to the other officer, "Maybe we should call him a cab?" One thing I learned in prison is you don't argue with the C.O's. They always win. I turned around and started to head back to my seat when he said, "Alright Cebula, I'll escort you back but you'll have to go to the yard instead of your cell. I thanked him and we left. (*"For whoever finds me finds life and receives favor from the Lord" (Proverbs* 8:35)

B-Block Yard

Within a few minutes I was out in the yard. There was another hour left for yard activity so I walked around the yard a few times looking for some friends. It was common to find a few guys sitting at one of the tables having a little Bible study but this day none were to be found. After walking around the yard a few times I found an unoccupied table and sat down. Having my Bible with me I opened it and began to read. It was hot and it was busy in the yard that day. Several hundred men in a small courtyard on a hot day was always a matter of concern. Although a few corrections officers were always present it would be extremely difficult to control the crowd if trouble did erupt. Sometimes fights between inmates would break out and officers seemed reluctant to get involved. Eventually they would break things up, but by that time there could be some serious injuries. As long as we were hurting each other and not them, they didn't seem to care. (Please don't misunderstand me. Many C.O.s are caring people but bad apples are found everywhere.) If you mind your own business you will be alright, but in Attica it doesn't always work that way. As I sat there with my Bible in hand I couldn't help thinking about the troubling things I heard in the church service. I was naive enough to believe a church service would never be the place to organize a strike.

Someone shouted out "Hey you! Come here!" I looked up and I saw a group of Hispanic guys motioning me over to them. Occasionally some of the guys would ask me to pray so I thought that's what they wanted. Boy was I ever wrong. As I approached them I suddenly found myself surrounded by as many as two dozen angry men. They were cursing, yelling and aggressively pointing at me as they pounded their fists into the palms of their hands. A few of them stood there with baseball bats in their hands and I quickly realized it wasn't to play baseball or hold a prayer service with me.

Because they were speaking in Spanish I didn't have a clue what was going on. All I knew was they were very angry at me and I was very scared. I was seconds away from having my head bashed in when one of the guys spoke out to me in English calling me a snitch. There's nothing worse than being called that in prison. Snitches don't usually live long in prison. They often become a "back door parole" (One who unexpectedly dies in prison). The prison code of "ethics" declares a snitch's behavior unacceptable. Not everyone survives the "snitch's beating". Why was I being called a snitch? I hadn't ratted out anyone. I couldn't believe this was happening to me. They were making a big mistake. With angry voices shouting and 24 pairs of eyes looking at me as their prey I shouted back to them, "You're wrong, you're wrong!" I didn't expect them to listen to me. It was already well past the point of reason.

Before I finish this story let me explain what brought about the false "snitch" accusation. (I found this out a few days later.) Remember where I was an hour or so earlier. I was in the Hispanic worship service when I heard of plans for an impending inmate strike. I decided to leave so I went to the back of the auditorium to get permission to leave. The other inmates saw me go back and talk to the C.O. They didn't know what I said but they assumed I was being a snitch because of the "favor" granted to me by the C.O. who allowed me to leave the service. Unknown to me (and unknown to them) there was a Spanish speaking C.O. that was listening to everything that was said about the strike. If they didn't nip this in the bud the entire prison population would be put in lock-down until things settled down. A "lock-down" is when inmates are confined to their cells for extended periods of time.

Meanwhile, as I was being escorted to the yard, the

riot squad came into the auditorium and quickly put an end to their meeting. The riot squad is a group of approximately 10 officers dressed in bright orange military type gear wearing gas masks, carrying clubs, tear gas canisters and other assault weapons. Their appearance alone is enough to stop a riot. As you can imagine they quickly put an end to the "meeting" and the inmates were escorted back to their cells and the organizers taken into SHU, the Special Housing Unit. We called it THE BOX. It was said by many inmates that the elevator going down to the BOX would often stop in-between floors if the C.O. wanted to "talk" to you for a few minutes. These "talks" usually left inmates with a few bruises from "accidents" that happened in the elevator.

As I mentioned earlier the prison grapevine travels fast. Within minutes the word was out in the B-Block recreation yard and the false allegations against me were being made. Those encircling me were about to carry out their assignment on my life. Unless it was stopped, I'd soon be "dancing on the pavement." (Left to die on the sidewalk) Almost miraculously for me, with little time remaining to deny their accusations, I saw their Hispanic group leader pushing his way through the angry mob. He approached me and pointed his finger directly into my face. I thought surely he was going be the first one to throw a punch. Instead, he looked squarely at me and said in clear English, "I know who you are. You're Phil. I've been watching you. You're a Christian and you tell the truth." He instantly turned around and walked away from me. All the others followed. I was left alone and was totally vindicated before my peers. The snitch label never stuck. Not only did I receive the favor of God, but I also had the favor of man.

That day I learned a valuable lesson; the importance of living an honest testimony before man. If I was faking my Christianity, I would not have survived the encounter. If others were not able to identify a glimpse of Jesus reflected in me, my life may have ended that day. I'm not perfect; no one is, but people do see when an honest effort is being made to walk the walk not just talk the talk. A Christian is not one whose life is a perfect reflection of Christ. We are all a work in progress daily depending on God's mercy and grace. It's not the size of the Bible I carry nor is it the number of times I attend church. Jesus living in my heart was not enough to satisfy my accusers. They had to see my faith evidenced in my actions.

# Chapter Thirteen

## C.O. in Trouble

*"But you, God, see the trouble of the afflicted; you consider their grief and take it in hand"*
*(Psalm 10:14a)*

There exists a differing between wisdom and knowledge or intelligence. The beginning of wisdom starts with the fear of the Lord. Although at times they may seem to complement each other quite often they are contradictory. Because God's ways are so different mankind will often reject the wisdom of God because it seems foolish. (*"As the heavens are higher than the earth, so are my ways higher than your ways, and my thoughts than your thoughts."* (*Isaiah 55:9*) We mistakenly accredit wisdom to man based upon his academic knowledge and longevity of life. That's where the mistake is often made. "Wisdom" must also be based upon a reliable source of knowledge. I am convinced that the best source of knowledge for gaining wisdom comes from the Holy Bible. In other words, the more time we spend reading and absorbing the word of God, the more Godly wisdom we acquire.

Much of my time in prison I spent reading and absorbing the Word of God. I often spent hour after hour with my Bible open as I studied God's Word. It was changing me on the inside. My way of thinking was becoming more in line with God's way. The knowledge I was receiving was transforming my thought life resulting in Godly wisdom. I began saying things that flowed from that wisdom. My thoughts were becoming more and more the thought patterns of God. As a result of this gained wisdom, inmates often sought me out for advice. I didn't have a certificate for counseling or a degree from any university. But what I did have was God's Word in my heart. If we are willing to receive the advice (wisdom) of His Word, our life can be changed. His wisdom penetrates the heart and makes a difference. *"For the word of God is alive and active. Sharper than any double-edged sword, it penetrates even to dividing soul and spirit, joints and marrow; it judges the thoughts and attitudes of the heart."* (*Hebrews 4:12*). As I read and studied the scriptures Godly wisdom was being deposited within me. I didn't know it was happening as much as others noticed it. I didn't ask for it but I was becoming a prison counselor.

Inmates spoke to me about serious matters. Some shared things with me that they had never shared with anyone before. Marriages in crisis, children going astray, anger issues, loneliness, and thoughts of suicide were some of the things we discussed. I never claimed to have the answers nor did I charade myself as a qualified counselor. My advice was usually quite simple. After listening to their story we would look at what the Bible said about their particular situation. This took the pressure off me and placed things into God's hands. Wisdom is when you know that you don't have the answers but God does. I didn't make promises, but I directed people to His promises. I didn't have profound advice to offer but as we read God's Word together advice was found. The comfort I offered as a friend was dwarfed by the comfort of the Holy Spirit. Many men gave their hearts to the Lord during these sessions. Suicidal thoughts were replaced with new desires to live. Discouraged men were discovering hope. Sometimes family relationships were restored. Occasionally inmates would ask family members to correspond with me for advice.

God's wisdom is powerful. If applied, it heals, directs, comforts, and gives hope.

One story stands out from them all. It's the story of a corrections officer who became my friend. This doesn't happen very often. It is clearly (understandably) frowned upon in the department of corrections. Officers can be (should be) friendly, but developing friendships are unprofessional and dangerous. Fraternizing with inmates could result in disciplinary action and or termination. As you might expect, our friendship was rather secretive.

C.O. Charlie (not his real name) was a typical officer about 40 years in age. He worked the second shift (3pm-11pm) and his assignment was usually in B-Block. He was friendly, professional and respected by most. Like most C.O.s he knew his job and understood the importance of maintaining a proper relationship between himself and the inmates. On occasion Charlie would bring troubled inmates to me for "counsel". He could see how God was helping others cope with their problems and always seemed genuinely concerned when he brought them to me. Sometimes when we were in the yard having one of our table Bible studies, he'd come by just to see how we were doing. He'd make comments like, "Glad to see you guys reading your Bibles" or "It sure doesn't hurt to pray." One day when I was sitting alone he stopped long enough for us to have a short conversation. He asked me about my faith and made a comment about the peace I seemed to be enjoying. "You're happier than some people I know on the outside. Keep the faith." Our conversation ended and he continued to walk his beat.

I sensed there was more to C.O. Charlie's brief table encounter. A few days later he did it again, and then again. Each time it was when I was alone and each encounter was a little longer and more revealing. I could see that he had problems and needed someone to talk to. I'm not sure why he had chosen me but as each meeting ended I knew more and more about his personal life. His marriage was in shambles, his wife wanted to leave him, and he didn't know what to do. He continued to share details of his personal life with me, a condition most at Attica would have considered unheard of. If other C.O.s knew what he was doing he would be ostracized by his own peers. If the department found out he would likely lose his job. We both knew the importance of keeping the meetings most discreet and confidential. Eventually I began to share my faith and the Scriptures with him. He was ready to hear it, and one evening in B-Block, Officer Charlie prayed with me and asked Jesus to come into his heart. It was a quick simple sinner's prayer.

We couldn't let others know what was happening. It had to remain our little secret. But it was no secret in heaven. C.O. Charlie was Born-Again and the angels rejoiced. His name was written down in the Lamb's book of life. He was now my "secret" brother. I encouraged him to buy a Bible and find a good church in his town. He said he would. Eventually our guard and prisoner relationship went back to normal. He wasn't stopping at my table any longer. Our conversations returned to being cordial and brief. He was once again C.O. Charlie, carrying out his responsibilities in B-Block. Every now and then he would pass by with a smile on his face and say, "Things are better these days, thanks Phil." Incredibly, over time I had witnessed C.O. Charlie being drawn to a position sufficient in trust to a prisoner (and one convicted of murder) for something greater in importance than job or career. He stepped out and somehow trusted that I would not violate this trust nor later expect any manner of favoritism. I never told anyone what happened.

**Early Years of Camping**

**Fifties Night**

**Ministering together in England**

**Spending time in the Holy Land**

**Down time in Haiti**

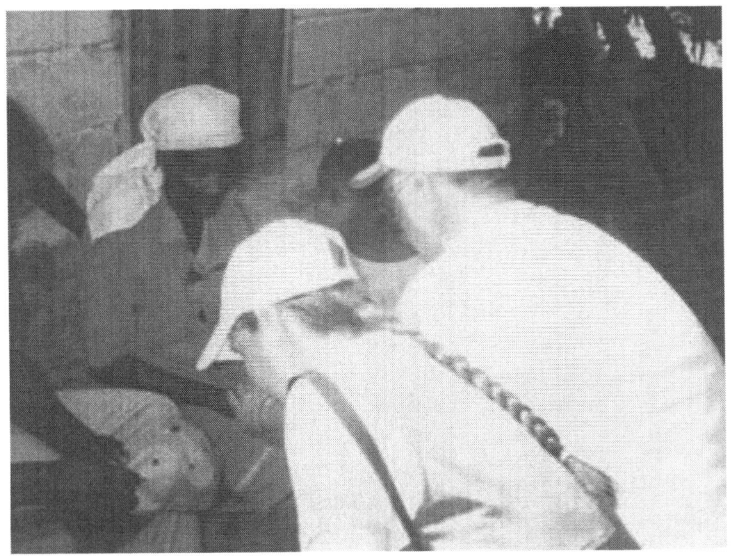

**Serving in Haiti**

The Boys "Bless the Food"

Jonah, Asante, Issaiah
Gavin, "Papa", and Ezekiel

**Our son Dan's Family**
**Beth, Dan, Gavin & Kennedy**

**Andrea, Jennifer, Daniel, and Cheryl**

# Chapter Fourteen

## Community Connections

"Remember those in prison as if you were their fellow prisoner...." *(Hebrews 13:3a)*

"***You've got Mail!***" It would usually take place in the afternoon. One of the C.O.s would stand at the entrance to your corridor and shout out the words, "Mail Call". My, how I loved to hear those words! With a stack of cards and letters in his hands he would begin walking down the aisle stopping at the cells of those who received mail. I was always expecting something in the mail so I would stand eagerly in front of my cell awaiting my turn. I didn't have to wait very long. I lived in cell #13, and within a few minutes the "mailman" would be standing in front of my house with a letter in his hand. Occasionally he would walk by saying, "Not today" and in disappointment I would sit down on the edge of my bunk telling myself tomorrow would be a better mail day. I was usually right. Most days I would receive mail or an occasional care package. My friends and family were always faithful; keeping me posted with events at home and in the outside world. They were my community connection. Never did I feel forgotten or abandoned in prison. I knew I was loved and others were thinking of me and praying for me.

With letter in hand I'd sit on my bed reading and re-reading my valuable community connection for the day. At times I would cry and other times I'd laugh. I celebrated their weddings and I mourned the loss of loved ones. Letters were always considered your lifeline with the outside world. Sometimes I'd read a letter so many times that I memorized it. When I read I would visualize faces and hear their voices as I tried to embrace the emotion of the writer. After reading I'd file it away to be read again. Again the next day I'd eagerly await the words, "Mail Call".

Most letters were of the personal nature but other times it would be appropriate to share them with others. Guys who seldom received mail always appreciated my sharing these letters with them. Occasionally they would ask me to "say Hi" to my friends, when I wrote them back. You can imagine how excited they would be when one of my friends said "Hi" back to them. One such remark led to an ongoing correspondence which developed into weekly visits, a proposal, and marriage. (Who would have thought?)

Although we had phone privileges, phone calls were very brief, infrequent, and expensive to those who accepted our long distance calls. Sometimes right in the middle of a conversation your time limit was up, and you were abruptly disconnected.

***The visiting room*** was the only other reliable connection we had with the outside world. Unlike letter correspondence in which you could initiate communication by writing first, your receiving a visit was solely dependent upon others. Simply put, if no one came to visit there wasn't anything you could do about it. I was fortunate to have visits every week. The visiting room in Attica was much better than the county jail. Visits would take place in a large room that easily accommodated 75-100 inmates plus their guest. When I first arrived in Attica the visiting room consisted of long tables in which you sat on one side and your visitor on the other. Visiting room conditions eventually improved. Long tables were replaced with round restaurant type tables and chairs allowing for a much more comfortable setting.

Once you were notified that visitors had arrived and were waiting for you, you'd quickly go back to your cell to spruce yourself up and put on your cleanest clothes. Every inmate had the same wardrobe of green pants, green shirt with your name and number over the pocket, and a pair of state issued sneakers. Before we could enter the visiting room we had to be frisked to make sure we weren't attempting to "fly a kite" (contraband letters). Sometimes we were told to strip down for a more thorough inspection. These searches included opening your mouth so the C.O. could gaze into it for drugs. As you stood there naked, your clothing was carefully inspected for approval. The most humiliating part of the search was being told to "bend over and spread your cheeks" as you were inspected in the place "*where the sun didn't shine*". I was never quite sure who was more humiliated by this procedure, inmates or officers conducting the inspection.

After clearing inspection you were safe and ready to enter the visiting room. Upon entering your eyes began to frantically search for a familiar face. With well over 100 people in the room, it wasn't always easy finding them. Quite often you didn't know who you were looking for. Eventually your eyes would meet theirs and an embrace or brief kiss would take place as you sat down and escaped the reality of prison life for the duration of your visit.

My parents were my most frequent visitors. Throughout my years of incarceration they were faithful to visit me on a weekly basis. I knew it was painful for them to see me in such a place yet they continued to come. I was told that often when visits ended it was not uncommon to find family members returning to the parking lot, bent over in emotional pain as they left their loved one in the prison behind them. I often wondered if my parents ever experienced this pain. I never asked. I didn't want to know the answer.

# *Twice Convicted*

Every visit was a cherished blessing, but there's one I will never forget. As I sat at the table talking to my Mom and Dad, we began to discuss my new found faith. Both my parents were solid Catholic. It was part of their heritage and they did their best to present their faith to me. As a family we went to Mass each week and participated in all aspects of our religion. As I shared earlier I drifted away from the church but not from my belief in God.

When I became a Born-Again Christian my parents were skeptical of my newfound faith. How could I leave the church that our family was so deeply rooted in? St. Hyacinth was my church and my school. There were no options! Why would I abandon all they taught me? "Once a Catholic, always a Catholic!" was the unspoken motto of the Polish community. We seldom talked about my faith. It was somewhat offensive to them. I was zealous and at times my enthusiasm would rub them the wrong way. They were not pleased with my departure from Catholicism, yet they were not critical of my choice; after all, Jesus was the central figure in both our beliefs. One thing they could not deny, I had peace.

One day in the visiting room, the much avoided topic came up. We began discussing my faith. I'm not sure who brought it up first but I do remember being very cautious with my words. I did not want to offend them. I had hurt them enough and I surely didn't want them to think I was being critical of the Catholic Church. As we talked they admitted noticing that I was at peace. They didn't understand how I could be experiencing peace of mind while in a place like Attica. As our conversation continued, I knew this was a unique moment that was orchestrated by God. It was time for me to be bold, so I said, "Mom, Dad, according to the Bible you must be Born-Again in order for you to enter the Kingdom of Heaven." An awkward silence settled in around the table.

Should I change the subject or should I follow up with more of the same? The door was open; should I shut it? I decided to proceed. I talked about their religion and how good it was, yet they needed much more than "religion"; they needed a relationship with God through Jesus. There I was teaching them about God. Would they stop me or allow me to speak. They continued to listen until finally I came to the part where I asked them if they were ready to ask Jesus to come into their heart. They said yes, and right there in the visiting room of Attica State Prison, I led my mother and father in the sinner's prayer as they received Jesus Christ into their hearts as Born Again believers in Christ. They always had a good solid church background, but on that day a personal relationship with the Lord was added to their religious experience. I occasionally get strange looks when I tell others that my parents were saved while in Attica Prison. On August 18, 1987 my father went home to be with the Lord. On December 24, 2009 my mother did the same. I plan on seeing them again.

# Chapter Fifteen

## It's all in the Cards

*"Fix these words of mine in your hearts and minds...."*
*(Deuteronomy 11:18a)*

I was growing in my Christian faith and becoming more and more aware of the importance of knowing God's Word. From the first time I read the Bible at the Erie County Jail in Buffalo, I realized the power God's Word had in making a difference in my life. Not only was I now reading the Bible more often, I also began listening to cassette tapes, Christian radio stations, reading faith-based books, and absorbing as much of the Word into me as possible. We didn't have TVs in our cells but occasionally there were opportunities to watch a TV evangelist on Sunday morning in one of the day rooms. Although the preachers did not always doctrinally agree with each other, there was one thing they did agree on; memorizing the Word of God was of great value. The psalmist declares, *"I have hidden your Word in my heart that I might not sin against you."* (*Psalm 119:11*). And *Joshua 1:8* tells us to, *"....meditate on it day and nig*ht........." I have always admired those who could flawlessly quote the Word of God from memory. It was time for me to do the same. I was determined to plant more of God's Word into my heart but first I needed to plant the seeds into my head. Memorization was my way of accomplishing this. Eventually my heart would benefit from it.

Where should I begin? What verses are the most important? Which ones do I memorize first? I decided to memorize some of the verses that I had highlighted in my Bible. Since it was late in the year, I decided to make it my New Year's resolution to memorize 52 verses in the coming year. Beginning January 1, 1977 I took my first step on this journey. I decided to begin with the most read verse of the Bible, *"For God so loved the world that He gave His one and only Son, that whoever believes in Him shall not perish but have eternal life. (John 3:16)* Every week I determined to memorize another verse until all 52 verses were part of my scriptural repertoire. I worked in the prison metal shop office and had access to a typewriter and 3x5 business cards so I began typing out each verse on a card until I had my deck of 52 cards.

I carried them around everywhere I could; reading them over and over until I felt confident enough to go on to the next. I admire those who have the ability to memorize whole chapters with very little effort, but for me it was a huge undertaking. It didn't come easy for me. The repetition was tedious yet I was determined to accomplish my goal. At times my attempt to memorize one verse would cause me to forget the verse from the week before. I can empathize with those who struggle with this. One step forward, two steps back. Week after week I worked on my cards until finally after several months I had my first 10 verses memorized.

Bill sat at the desk to the right of me in the metal shop office. He was convicted of murdering both his parents in the early 1970's in a posh neighborhood of Long Island, New York. He was sentenced to life in prison. I wondered what caused him to snap and commit such a violent crime. Very few inmates talked freely about the details of their conviction. The unwritten rule of the prison system is, don't ask; it's none of your business. Eventually Bill did open up to me and shared how he was repeatedly molested by both his parents. Like so many others Bill didn't seem like the type of guy who belonged in prison. He was educated, quiet, gentle, and courteous. His manners were clearly a reflection of his proper upbringing. He was always polite yet he made it very clear that he didn't want to be bothered with any of the "Bible stuff". He described himself as an Agnostic who was seriously considering joining the ranks of Atheism.

We had some lively office discussions yet Bill would always make it very clear that he was not a candidate for conversion. I think he wanted to convert me to his camp. I was still a young believer. One could even suggest perhaps still a baby Christian. Bill was an educated man, well degreed, very mentally agile, and surely able to present strong arguments against the existence of God. With far greater maturity now I realize if that which I had at that time would have come from only man, Bill might have been able to prevail because his debating skills and his arguments were so strong. But that which I had was given to me from God and, thus no man could touch it. At times I didn't know how to respond and he would win the argument for that day. A typical day at the office would always include one of these discussions. At the end of the work day neither one of us was persuaded by the other. With a smile on our faces we went back to our cells unchanged. The next day would be the same. Some things seem impossible but with God all things are possible. I didn't have all the answers but three things I did have: my testimony, my deck of cards and a gift of faith that was anchored in God.

Day after day I sat at my desk shuffling through my deck, reading and re-reading them in my attempt to memorize the scriptures. Bill would occasionally look my way with an inquisitive eye until one day he asked me what

I was reading. I showed him my cards and told him how I had set a goal to memorize 52 verses. "Why bother?" he asked. "Is it that necessary?" I told him it wasn't necessary but it was beneficial. I was always looking for the opportunity to share my faith with him, so I continued my conversation by saying "God is changing me little by little through these cards." I said I didn't know how it worked, but these Scriptures brought me strength, comfort, and peace even in a place like Attica Prison. "How are you doing with memorizing them?" he asked. "Not that great. I'm not good at this memorization stuff. It seems to be taking me forever to learn just a few of them." I mentioned how I read and re-read, how I meditated on them, and how I was even writing the verses down over and over. "Have you tried reading them out loud?" he said, "Reciting always helped me in college. Let me have those cards. I'll give you the reference and you quote it back to me." It sounded like a good plan, or should I say a GOD plan. I handed him the deck of cards. The Word of God was now in Bill's hands.

Bill was right. Reciting the verses made it so much easier to memorize them. "What does Romans 3:23 say? "What does 2Timothy 2:15 say?" "How about Hebrews 11:1?" And so it went. He gave me the scripture reference and I would do my best to quote it properly. Every time I misquoted he was quick (yet polite) to correct me. Day after day this became part of our routine. We'd pour ourselves some coffee and then Bill would ask, "Are you ready to do the cards?" I think he was a little bit uncomfortable using the word "Bible"; it was always "Do the cards". As we continued with the flash cards, faith was rising up inside of me. Scripture declares, "Consequently, faith comes from hearing the message; and the message is heard through the word of Christ." (*Romans 10:17*) As I read each verse out loud my faith was increasing. But I wasn't the only one being affected by the cards.

# *It's All in the Cards*

The heart of a borderline Atheist was being softened by the truth of Scripture. God's Word has the power to do that! "*For the word of God is living and active. Sharper than any double-edged sword, it penetrates, even to the dividing soul and spirit, joints and marrow; it judges the thoughts and attitudes of the heart.*" (Hebrews 4:12) Right before my eyes his heart was being softened. Then it started. Bill began asking me questions pertaining to the cards that I quoted. "Does God love me? Can I still be forgiven? What is mercy? What is grace? What does it mean to be Born-Again?" When I was selecting the memory verses and typing them onto those 3x5 cards little did I know just how carefully the Holy Spirit was leading me with each verse selection. With every verse I quoted, Bill had questions. My memorization sessions were rapidly turning into Bible studies. Eventually Bill heard enough and he was ready to make his decision. I invited him to our next Bible study and it was there that he gave his heart to the Lord. God used those 3x5 cards to reach a man who thought he was unlovable. Doubt and skepticism were replaced with desire and a hunger for the truth. It was personally rewarding to watch God change Bill's life and see him become an active part of our prison church. The Bible that he once rejected was now his embraced companion. It was all a part of God's plan. It was all in the cards. I don't remember if I accomplished my goal of 52 verses, but one thing I know, it was enough to see Bill's life changed.

# Chapter Sixteen

## Seven Acorns.... the planting of the Lord

*"Praising God and enjoying the favor of all the people; And the Lord added to their number daily those who were being saved."* (Acts 2:47)

**A**s previously mentioned, my first encounter with the prison church was a meeting in a small class room for Friday evening Bible study with seven inmates in attendance (including myself). We were relatively satisfied with our accommodations, considering the fact that we still had room for another dozen. Sunday services were always held in our huge auditorium with plenty of empty seats, but it was on Friday nights that our revival was most noticed. One by one the church began growing. Although un-noticed at the time, God had strategically placed committed believers throughout the confines of the prison. His "fishers of men" were leading other inmates to the Lord in every corner of Attica. *"But you will receive power when the Holy Spirit comes on you; and you will be my witnesses in Jerusalem, and in all Judea and Samaria, and to the ends of the earth." (Acts 1:8)* The ends of the earth at that time were A-block, B-block, C-block, D-block, and E-block; and all were being evangelized by men who had their lives turned around by a loving forgiving Savior. God was raising leaders who were boldly proclaiming His Word to set the prisoners "free". Reports were coming in on the prison grapevine that hardened criminals were shedding tears of joy as they surrendered their lives to God.

I can't help but wonder if the Attica Riot had played a part in the revival that hit the prison. I can only speculate but I truly believe that this painfully tragic event not only raised awareness of unacceptable prison conditions, but it also was bringing many believers to their knees as they prayed for the men behind its wall. Reports were beginning to come in of prayer groups throughout the state (and beyond) that were seeking God and asking Him to send a revival into Attica. Christian volunteerism began increasing and letter writing campaigns began as area churches encouraged their members to find a prison pen-pal and share the Gospel with them. God was in the midst of turning this tragedy into a triumph for His glory. Prison ministries such as Chaplain Ray's International Prison Ministry and Chuck Colson's Prison Fellowship were sprouting up across America.

You may recall that Chuck Colson was special counsel to President Nixon and was implicated in the Watergate Scandal that shook this nation in the early 1970's. Known as the "Hatchet Man" he was eventually convicted of Obstruction of Justice charges and was sentenced to serve a maximum of three years in the Maxwell Federal Correctional Facility in Alabama. Disgraced publically, yet embraced personally by Jesus Christ, Mr. Colson became a Born-Again Christian. "Time" magazine ridiculed his conversion but God used it to His glory. The "Hatchet Man" had become "God's Herald" as his life changing testimony touched the lives of multitudes. He served only seven months of his sentence and shortly after his release founded "Prison Fellowship", a ministry that continues its great impact on prisoners, their families, and society. I'll never forget Chuck Colson's authoritative voice and his heartfelt compassion when he visited our facility and shared his testimony and God's Word with us. As one of the church's seven inmate deacons I had the honor of eating lunch with both Mr. Colson and Chaplain Ray in our cafeteria when they came to minister in our prison.

Weekly radio broadcasts were informing their listeners of the good news that was spreading behind the walls of notorious prisons. Testimony books were published and freely distributed into the hands of thousands of inmates resulting in a multitude of changed lives. Bibles, that at one time were scarce, were becoming much more available to inmates. In the 1970's a revival that would become known as "The Charismatic Movement" was spreading across our land and was making its way to the walls of our prisons. Nothing could stop this mighty move of God as it penetrated the maximum security prisons of America. Attica wasn't the only prison where this move of God was having results but it sure seemed to be a strong catalyst for prison revival across America.

The church behind the walls was growing and our Friday group soon found itself overflowing into the hall. What a blessing it was seeing new believers added to the church each week. The size of our small class room, piano and pulpit included, was no longer adequate. With two dozen men in the room and another dozen in the hall, a need for more space was obvious. Within a few weeks we moved into a larger classroom with a capacity for fifty. With everyone out of the hallway the church was together again and the power and presence of God was faithful to meet with us every week. But the church was still adding in numbers daily and soon our new larger room would again be filled and overflowing. One would think that a growing prison church population would make the department of corrections happy. Not necessarily. Added inmates in a room would always call for added security. The need of one officer to cover seven inmates had rapidly increased to three or four needed for fifty inmates and growing. Moving officers from one place in the prison to provide security in another place always leaves a "risk area". The dilemma was temporarily solved by dividing the Friday Bible study into two groups. Cell blocks A and B would meet one week; C, D, and the smaller Block E would meet the next. This alternating system helped resolve the security issue but it left the church fragmented……and still growing.

Eventually we filled the room again, overflowing into the hallway each week. Collectively our "Friday Church" had grown to approximately one hundred and fifty………and was still growing! We were learning the value of prayer and the power it had to make a difference. The church started praying for a larger room and within a few short weeks God met our need. There's a gymnasium in Attica with folding bleachers, and that became our new church home. It takes a lot to quiet the sound of bouncing basketballs in a prison gym. For some, shooting hoops was the highlight of the week. There could have been resentment and tension from those inmates who didn't want to give up their gym night…….but God was in the mix. Eventually all were satisfied when those in authority assigned a different night for basketball and other gym activities. Week after week, month after month, the bleachers were rolled out and the church came together to hear the Word of the Lord. We loved to sing praises to God. One of the inmates named Don wrote a song that eventually became our Friday Night theme song. With guitar in hand he'd lead us and we sang.

**Roll Away**

(written by Don, a former Attica Inmate)

I got down on my knees and I prayed
To the Lord that my soul would be saved
He has answered all my prayers

He took my sins and all of my cares
Yes the Lord has rolled the stone of sin away

Roll away (echo....Roll away)
Roll away (echo....Roll away)
Yes the Lord has rolled the stone of sin away
He has answered all my prayers
He took my sins and all of my cares
Yes the Lord has rolled the stone of sin away

I asked Jesus from this prison to be free
He said praise me and I will satisfy your need
He will open up those doors
You will walk on golden shores
Yes the Lord will roll the prison doors away

Roll away (echo....Roll away)
Roll away (echo....Roll away)
Yes the Lord will roll the stone of doubt away
Anytime you are in doubt,
Get on your knees and shout it out
Yes the Lord will roll the stone of doubt away.

The church kept growing both numerically and spiritually. Our chaplains and the outside volunteers taught us well. Each week they imparted the truths of Scripture without compromise. They were teaching us the value of God's Word and instructing us in the way of the Lord. We were becoming grounded and rooted in our faith as they ministered to our hearts, not just to our heads. The weekly Bible studies were impacting lives. Many salvations, healings, and deliverances were taking place. Often men would come to these meetings by personal invitation or simply out of curiosity, but before being escorted back to their cells many of them were truly touched by the hand of God and were born again. The Bible studies always ended as we prayed for each other and for our families.

The church was alive and well. There was freedom behind the walls of Attica. It was Friday night in prison and it was exciting. For ninety minutes it felt as if we were somewhere else. Don't misunderstand me but I sure do hold to the memory dearly. We were for the moment in a different place. We were in the presence of the Lord. The church kept growing and before very long the gym became too small for us. We ended up with our Friday night services being held in the prison auditorium where we had plenty of room for church expansion. It started with seven small acorns but it soon became a mighty oak tree. *"They will be called oaks of righteousness, a planting of the Lord for the display of His splendor." (Isaiah 61:3)*

# Chapter Seventeen

## Chink in the Armor

*"Too long have I lived among those who hate peace"*
*(Psalm 120:6)*

My first experience of a Christmas holiday in prison came just seven months after my incarceration in Attica. On Christmas Eve, for the first time, I heard the groans of prisoners feeling the pain of separation from their loved ones. Hardened criminals are not supposed to cry but sometimes they do and sometimes it's acceptable. Typically the only sounds one would hear in the nightly hours were cell soldiers (one who talks tough when locked in his cell) or the repetitious sounds of snoring. This night was very different. Locked up in the darkness of their prison cell some inmates grieved in pain and remorse as they tried to deal with incarceration at Christmas. Pillows muffled their curses and quieted their screams but changed nothing. Some didn't care who heard them, they just let it out. This was a time when thoughts of family rise to a place almost unbearable. Hearts are wrenched in pain as their minds are outside the walls but physically they remain within. They know their families will be celebrating together, unwrapping presents and eating turkey dinners. The children will be opening presents from daddy but daddy would be absent. Although you try to fight off these depressing thoughts, your mind keeps rehearsing them over and over until it can be borne no longer. Occasionally one of the C.O.s would walk down the corridor attempting to hush up the hurting inmates but not much could be done to silence the pain. I discovered that suicides and attempted suicides would increase during special family days such as this.

As I listened that night and pondered the "sounds of the season" I empathized with their pain and misery. Their behavior was completely understandable. It was then I realized that my feelings were completely different and I found myself questioning why I wasn't feeling the pain of the holidays. I thought there's nothing wrong with what I was hearing. I was spending my first Christmas in prison, my wife had filed for a divorce, and I was separated from my family and friends. I should be disheartened! I should be crying! I should be lonely! Only a sociopath would feel the way I did, disconnected from the pain. It's normal to hurt like they were. It's abnormal not to.

I wondered, was I abnormal and didn't know it? Could I be losing my mind? These thoughts were racing through my mind as I lay there listening to the cries of "sound-minded men". Don't misunderstand me, not everyone was up that night. Most were sound asleep escaping reality for the moment. But not me, I wasn't crying nor was I asleep. Instead I was questioning my sanity. How does a person know if they are mentally unstable? If I were, would it prevent me from understanding my condition? Much like those with Alzheimer's who do not even realize they have the disease.

This was not a fleeting thought. Into the night I questioned my mental condition. It was frightening to even consider the possibility that I might be losing my mind. I was incarcerated on Christmas Eve yet I was at peace. I was the odd duck that night. They were normal and I was abnormal. At times I was actually smiling. Now that scared me! Was I really at peace or did I disconnect from reality?

The cries and groans continued to echo down the corridor as I lay there in my stupor. Before the night was over the answer to the question of my sanity would be revealed. That night was to become a defining moment in my Christian growth. The hours passed and it was now almost 2 am. I tried to fall asleep, but to no avail. I was restless and confused about my sanity. By now the halls had quieted down, but sleep was still elusive for me. I finally decided to take my concerns to God. Why do we wait so long to pray? The hymn writer (Joseph Scriven) nailed it in 1855 when he penned the words of the ever popular "What a Friend We Have In Jesus; What a privilege to carry everything to God in prayer. Oh, what peace we often forfeit. Oh, what needless pain we bear; All because we do not carry everything to God in prayer." Sitting on the edge of my bunk, I quietly sought out the Lord's voice for an answer. It wasn't a long wait! Within minutes He spoke to me through one of the verses I had memorized. *"Do not be anxious about anything, but in everything, by prayer and petition, with thanksgiving, present your request to God. (7) And the peace of God, which transcends all understanding, will guard your hearts and your minds in Christ Jesus." (Philippians 4:6-7)*

BAM! The truth of that Scripture hit me and instantly settled the question of my sanity. I began to silently rejoice. I couldn't explain it then and I can't fully explain it today, but His peace was flowing through me like a river. My doubts rapidly vanished. I wasn't supposed to comprehend it because it was *"beyond understanding"*. I didn't have to understand to appreciate it. I thanked the Lord for this marvelous revelation of truth that He deposited into my heart in the early hours of Christmas day. Before long I drifted off into a peaceful night's sleep embracing the gift of peace that God had imparted into me. Probably still with a smile on my face.

# *Twice Convicted*

Things were much different after that night. The inner awareness of His peaceful presence catapulted me to another level of my daily walk. The *"joy of the Lord"* daily became my strength as I continued to carry out my charge as His ambassador in this dark place. With renewed strength comes boldness and confidence. No longer was I simply doing my time in prison, for I now had my assignment and was invigorated with an increasing desire to carry out my mission. Fresh deposits of God's glory were daily being poured into my spirit as the maturation process continued. Although far from mature I was no longer a babe in Christ. It was 18 months since I was born-again and I was now chasing the deeper truths of Scripture, the meat. Milk sustains us, but it is the meat of God's Word that brings us to maturity. *"Anyone who lives on milk, being still an infant is not acquainted with the teachings about righteousness. But solid food is for the mature, who by constant use have trained themselves to distinguish good from evil."* (*Hebrews 5:13-14*)

Maturing is not easy and it's not instant. Most of the changes that were taking place would not be easily discernible by others; they were "inner" changes. The developing of Christ-like character and integrity takes place within one's heart. In due time these changes will better establish who you are, but until such a time your outward appearance is the same. The fruit of the Spirit will eventually blossom, but the onset of your walk leaves others questioning the sincerity of your faith. My inner peace however was now being evidenced to others. Good news, right? Not necessarily so! Not everyone in Attica wanted to see me happy. Some resented the fact that I had peace and they lacked it. I would soon find out that jealousy, if not properly addressed can lead to rage, and rage can harm. *"Too long have I lived among those who hate peace." (Psalm 120:6)*

## *Chink in the Armor*

I wasn't aware of his animosity concerning me but eventually I would find out that Wayne (not his real name) was one harboring such jealousy. His jealousy had grown to a place of hatred and he determined that one day he would "shank me". A shank, also called a "shiv" is a prison term for a hand-made knife. Day after day I'd nod my head and say "Hi". Day after day he looked for his opportunity to harm me. I occasionally extended an invitation for him to join us at our Friday Bible study, but his response was always the same, "Not today, I'm not ready for that Bible stuff." He always appeared friendly, so I never gave it a second thought that he wanted to harm me. I persisted with my invitations even though they always seemed to fall on deaf ears. But God was working behind the scene. Not only was God protecting me from harm, He was also softening Wayne's heart in preparation to meet Him.

One day when I invited him, his response was different, "Not today, maybe next time." There it was; a chink in the armor. His resistance was beginning to break down by my unknowing persistence and was resulting in the softening of his heart by the Holy Spirit. Active faith has its rewards and Wayne's salvation in time would be rewarding to me. I felt by then it was only a matter of time before he would respond to my Friday night invitation. I had seen it happen in others. It's exciting when you can see the fruition of your efforts. A few more invites, a few more chinks. "Hey Wayne, today's Friday, how about joining us for Bible study?" I waited a few seconds for his response. "I guess so; I'll be there. I've got nothing better to do. I'll see you there, but just this one time!"

Pastor Farrington was our chaplain that night, and I clearly remember the topic of his sermon message, "Forgiveness". I glanced at Wayne out of the corner of my eye. He was not showing any signs that the message was speaking to his heart. He just sat there, expressionless until the very end. Pastor Farrington gave an altar call and Wayne responded, humbly asking the Lord to come into his heart. That night Wayne was Born-Again.

A few minutes later, he came over to me and asked me to forgive him. "Forgive you for what?" I asked. "You never did anything to me." He then told me the whole story of how he had hatred toward me and that many times he stood waiting for me to come around some corner so he could shank me or club me with a baseball bat or hurt me in some way. He wanted me dead or seriously injured, but God protected me. "Forgive me for what I was planning to do to you." he said. We shook hands as I assured him of my forgiveness. "But why were you angry with me?" I asked. "What did I ever do to you? Why did you want to hurt me?" I'll never forget his response. "Because you had peace, and I didn't. I envied that. It didn't seem fair, but tonight I found the same peace that you have. Now I have it too." Wayne continued attending on Friday Nights. He became my friend and my brother in Christ.

# Chapter Eighteen

## Tuna Fish Testimony

*""A time to weep, a time to laugh...."*
*(Ecclesiastes 3:4a)*

From many of the prior chapters in this book, one could arrive at the conclusion that Attica was a place of nonstop challenge and risk. That of course would be total folly, for not every day of prison life is filled with relentless severity. There were many prison activities to take the edge off prison life such as sports, films, and a wide variety of programs. Humorous events could also be found if one was determined to find it. The following parody will relate one of many such incidents in my prison life.

One evening around 7pm, as I was sitting in my cell, I heard a gentle tap on my metal wall coming from my next door neighbor in cell #12. It was Lucas, a Christian brother, a man serving a rather lengthy sentence for armed robbery. He was a very kind man, soft spoken and gentle. Although he was illiterate, he knew the content of his Bible. His love for God was noticeable and as a result he eventually became a deacon in our prison church. The next ten minute encounter with Lucas would prove to be very funny. Here's how it went down.

**Lucas:** Knock....knock.... "Hey Phil, I'm making myself a tuna sandwich and I'd like to put in some chopped onions. I'm completely out of onions, can I borrow one?"

**Me:** "Sure thing Luke"

**Lucas:** "Thanks Phil"..... (A short pause then) "Hey Phil I can't find my can opener for the tuna fish, can I borrow your can opener?"

**Me:** "Sure"

**Lucas:** "Thanks Phil" ...... (Another short pause and then) "Oh man, I just realized that I'm out of mayonnaise......can I borrow a little of yours?

**Me:** "Sure Lucas. Are you all set now?

**Lucas:** "Yep, I'm all set to eat. Thanks for the mayo." Another short pause then, Knock, knock, "Hey Phil you're not going to believe this but I can't find my bowl to mix up the tuna and mayo. You don't happen to have a bowl that I can borrow do you?

**Me:** "Yes I do Luke. Enjoy your sandwich."

**Lucas:** "Thanks again, I sure do appreciate it!"

By now I'm sure you realize that although Lucas is a nice guy, his mind operates differently. (No disrespect intended)

**Lucas:** Tapping on my wall again, "Hey Phil, how you doing over there? Hate to bother you again but my bread has mold on it so I can't use it. Do you have a few slices I can borrow? Actually four slices would be good. I'm making two sandwiches."

**Me:** "No Lucas, it's not a problem. Is there anything else I can do for you?" (Said sarcastically)

**Lucas:** "Nope. I sure do appreciate all this. Have a good night"

**Me:** "Enjoy"

(The entire cell corridor had become quiet as all ears are now listening in on our conversation.)

**Lucas**: "I think I'm all set now brother Phil. (pause) Wait a minute; I can't find my spoon to mix it up. Can I borrow yours? I'll give it right back. And one more thing and that's all.....do you have any lettuce? I'd like to put some on my sandwich"

**Me:** "OK here it comes" (Note: occasionally we were able to take leftover salad and other food items back to our cells from the prison dining hall.)

**Pause**

**Lucas:** **"**Hey Phil......do you have a...a."

**Me:** I know, I know. You probably need a couple paper plates for your sandwich. Here's a couple just in case you might need them. (Again, sarcastically) Enjoy your two sandwiches.

**Lucas:** "Actually I do need them. I'm all out of paper plates. Thanks, Phil"

**Long pause** (this time about 3-4 minutes)

**Lucas:** "Thanks brother. I've had my appetite set on a tuna sandwich with lettuce and onions all day long. But there's still one thing I need. I've looked everywhere and I can't find my can of tuna fish. Can I borrow a can of **tuna fish?"**

Immediately my good friend Mike (in cell #11) chimed in "Lucas, do you want Phil to cut it up for you and feed you?" At this, the entire block, me included, broke out in hysterical laughter. I thought he would have offered me one of his two sandwiches, but I was wrong. He must have been hungry and I'm sure he enjoyed them. Like I said about Lucas, his mind operated differently and that's just how the story unfolded and it was to the enjoyment of the whole cell block. Thus ended the "Tuna Fish Testimony."

# Chapter Nineteen

## Heart's Desire

*"Blessed is the one who reads aloud the words of this prophecy...." (Revelation 1:3a)*

There were more than ample humorous events in our prison lives which would not only make life easier and more tolerable, but offer opportunities to develop genuine camaraderie.

A typical day in Attica would usually include an opportunity for yard time. Activities in the yard included lifting weights, playing cards, checkers, chess, or a board game, watching TV, walking, jogging, or just simply relaxing out in the fresh air. For me it was an opportunity to be a part of a small group Bible study. That's where you would usually find me along with five or six other Christians. With our Bibles opened we eagerly studied the scriptures. We didn't have a designated group leader for these sessions yet we always had orderly discussions. We selected a portion of scripture to read and then talked about what we believed it meant and how it spoke to our hearts. None of us were Biblical scholars yet looking back on those days I am still amazed at how deep and theologically accurate many of our Bible studies were. When "teachers" are not available to teach, the Holy Spirit will provide truth to those who sincerely hunger for it. *"As for you, the anointing you received from Him remains in you, and you do not need anyone to teach you. But as His anointing teaches you about all things and as that anointing is real, not counterfeit, just as it has taught you, remain in Him." (1John 2:27)*

Some were better readers than others yet each eagerly participated when it was their turn to read. The only exception to this was Carlos. Carlos would always remind us that he could not read. It was not unlike him to ask me to read his mail to him. His problem is not uncommon in America's prisons. Studies have shown that approximately 20% of all inmates are illiterate. The average education level is sixth-grade.

Whenever it was his turn to read the Bible Carlos would reluctantly pass saying, "I'm sorry guys, but you know I can't read." We'd all assure him that it was OK and not to feel ashamed, yet his countenance and tone of voice always reflected embarrassment and shame. He so desperately wanted to read the Word of God. Oftentimes Carlos would say something like, "Someday I'll do it! Someday I won't have to pass the Bible. Someday I'll read it." Our response was comforting and reassuring to him as we would prayerfully come into agreement with the desire of his heart and collectively say, "Amen."

Our recreation yard Bible studies eventually became a routine part of my time in Attica Prison. Our group was hungry for the deeper truths of His Word. Friday night Bible study and Sunday morning services were not enough. Day by day God was changing us into His image as we continued to study His Scriptures. *"Like newborn babies, crave pure spiritual milk, so that by it you may grow up in your salvation." (1Peter 2:2)* All six of us were committed to meet as often as possible. And although Carlos would reluctantly pass on the Bible reading, he was growing in his faith because he was **hearing** the Word. "Consequently, *faith comes from hearing the message...." (Romans 10:17a)*

As Carlos' faith was growing, so was his desire to read. The Bible says, *"Take delight in the Lord, and He will give you the desires of your heart." (Psalm 37:4)*

His heart's desire was soon to be realized. One day when it was his turn to read he didn't say, "I'll pass", but instead he paused and said, "I'll read." Was he serious? But before we had a chance to question him Carlos began to read.....and read....and...read. Typically one would read a paragraph or a few verses and then stop to discuss the passage but not this time. Carlos read for what seemed to be 10 minutes and finally stopped. Although he didn't read eloquently he did read miraculously. When we asked him about it he simply said, "I've been asking the Lord for the ability to read and I figured it was time to step out in faith."

As you can imagine we were all excited. We witnessed a miracle that day. God gave Carlos the desire of His heart. Never again would he have to pass the Bible to someone else. Never again would he look at the pages and wonder what God was saying. Never again would he be ashamed. Later on we found out that God had also gifted him with the ability to read in Spanish. I'm not sure where Carlos is today but I do believe that wherever he is, you will find him using his miraculous gift to bring glory to the Lord. *"On that day the Book of Moses was read aloud in the hearing of the people......" (Nehemiah 13:1a)*

# Chapter Twenty

## The Kufi and the Koran

*"Those who find me find life*
*and receive favor from the Lord"*
*(Proverbs 8:35)*

Almost three years had passed since I first walked through the infamous front gate of Attica Prison. Unlike many others that had become hardened and embittered by prison life, my incarceration was proving to be surprising to me. Although undeserved, I felt the favor of the Lord was upon my life. His watchful eye of guidance and protection continually kept me out of harm's way. *"In all your ways submit to Him and he will make your paths straight." (Proverbs 3:6)* There were numerous times when I was about to go to the mess hall or out into the recreation yard and I would discern the inner voice of God instructing me not to go but rather to remain in my cell. I eventually realized these promptings were God's protection over my life as fights and inmate disturbances would often break out in the places I was planning to go before I changed my mind. Fighting is common in prison yet God always kept me at a safe distance from these altercations. Sometimes tear gas canisters were used to quell these incidents.

His hand upon my life was clearly noticeable in my relationships with others as well. I found favor with most inmates, corrections officers, administration personnel, and staff. Gaining favor with officers was normally viewed with great suspicion by other inmates. Most thought that only a snitch would have the favor of C.O.s and the administration. Whites were not always welcomed into the inner circle of friendships with Blacks, Hispanics, and other ethnic groups, but I always felt I was accepted. Much to my surprise as an unapologetic Christian I even experienced respect from within the growing Muslim Community in Attica.

Salim was one such follower of Allah. He shared with me how he was raised in a strong Christian home, sang in the youth choir, and recited his memory verses for his Sunday school teachers. Yet somewhere in his rebellious adolescent years he abandoned the faith of his family and attached himself to a life of crime in the streets of New York City. Poverty in the big city often leads young men and women in the wrong direction. With welfare and unemployment seemingly predicting his future, he decided to find what he called "a good paying job." His choice of profession: Drug Dealer. Good money, bad choice. He boasted of being very successful at it until the day he was arrested. His life of crime came to an abrupt end when he was convicted of the sale and distribution of an illegal substance (heroin, cocaine, and a variety of amphetamines), and was sentenced under the Rockefeller Drug Law to life in prison. At that time, New York State had the strictest anti-drug legislation in the country; if convicted, mandatory life in prison.

While in prison Salim became a devoted follower of Islam. He was a disciplined man in his pursuit of wisdom, knowledge, and a deeper understanding of his faith. Although our religious beliefs differed greatly we became friends. As a result we often held Bible/Koran discussions in our attempts to convert each another to our way of thinking. He would frequently invite me to attend his Muslim prayer services with him. I always politely declined. I also would invite him to attend our Friday night Bible study. His hunger for the truth would occasionally lead him to attend wearing his Kufi (prayer cap head covering) and carrying both his Bible and his Koran in his hand. For the next several months Salim struggled in his quest for truth.

He attended our Friday night services but also continued attending his Muslim prayer services. Salim's great hunger for truth would eventually lead him to the real Bread of Life. On this night, the Lord knocked again on the door of Salim's heart and he opened it for good.

With Bible in hand his struggle was finally settled. Salim would take off his Kufi and lay down his Koran for the final time. *"Here I stand at the door and knock. If anyone hears my voice and opens the door, I will come in and eat with that person and they with me." (Revelation 3:20 NIV) "And you will know the truth and the truth will set you free." (John 8:32)*

# Chapter Twenty-One

## The Blame Game

*"Then I acknowledged my sin to you and did not cover up my iniquity. I said, "I will confess my transgressions to the Lord." And you forgave the guilt of my sin."*
*(Psalm 35:5)*

**O**n July 19, 1975 I confessed my sinful nature to God and received His gracious forgiveness. I was Born-Again and that day was the beginning of my new life, a journey that would lead me down the path of His will rather than my own. By late 1978, the maturity of my life was well in progress. My desires and actions were becoming more in line with God's will for my life. Becoming like Him is not the result of a single decision but rather a lifelong commitment to follow after Him. The fact that God was using me in Attica prison made my incarceration more bearable. Please don't misunderstand me. I wanted out! That day would eventually come, but until then I was determined to serve the Lord inside the walls.

Forgiveness is a gift from God. When I first confessed my sinful nature and accepted His gift of forgiveness my sins were instantly and completely forgiven; the slate was wiped clean. The excitement was real. I still remember the feeling of heavenly joy as I danced around in my living room that special evening. The burden of sin was lifted and the peace of God had captured my heart as the fragrance of His presence filled the room. It had been a wonderful moment but something was still lacking.

# *Twice Convicted*

Although I had asked the Lord to forgive me I feared my remorse had been shallow. Tears of repentance did not flow that night as the contrition of my heart was void of genuine expression. Perhaps much like my "Act of Contrition" prayer I said in the confessional booth of the Catholic Church, it was void of deep repentance. That night God had indeed forgiven me, yet some time would pass before I was able to fully grasp the seriousness of my sin.

As a child I remember my mother saying "Tell your sister you're sorry." **"I'M SORRY!"** would be my reluctant half hearted response. And in turn my mother would say, "**Say it like you mean it**." In some ways I was concerned that my early repentance could have been similar. I was indeed sorrowful but I was sorry that I got caught. I was sorry for selfish reasons. I was sorry that I would have to suffer for my foolishness. I was very shallow with my sorrow. I regretted many of the choices that I made, but sorrow and remorse were yet to be experienced. Yes, God had forgiven me, but a deeper level of remorse was yet to be manifested in my life. God is quick to forgive and His forgiveness is always deeper than our remorse. It would take some time before I could, "Say it like I meant it."

When caught with your hand in the cookie jar it is so easy justifying ourselves by placing some or all of the blame on others. "Why did you put that cookie jar in front of me? You knew I'd be tempted." This type of transference often leaves us carrying unnecessary baggage that can stunt our Christian growth and slow down the maturation process in our lives. Justification is a common theme among most prisoners. The "Blame Game" is popular. It is easy for one to find others to blame for our imprisonment. Our attorney, the cops, our parents, our friends, our need for money, our addiction, the war in Viet-Nam, and "the devil made me do it" are some of the common justifiers of the incarcerated.

# *The Blame Game*

Seldom do you meet someone who accepts full responsibility for their actions. With constant exposure to this type of rhetoric it is easy to allow others to become our alibi, and I found myself beginning to slip into this Blame Game mental state. I had my list of excuses for being where I was. I played the "Blame Game" and I played it well. Yes, I did acknowledge my sin but I always felt that others were more to blame than me. This of course shallows the depth of remorse and minimizes the necessity for genuine repentance. This kind of baggage can create problems for you in the future. To ignore the condition is to ignore a cancer that can lead to crime repetition or other serious problems. A time would finally come when my soul compelled me to face the music, to face the man in the mirror.

Inmates are always telling their story and blame is commonly woven throughout each episode. After hearing countless accounts I began to notice the common thread, blame. Shame and responsibility were noticeably absent from these stories. Often I would question the story teller about their failure to admit they were wrong. I thought, "They don't get it! They don't see what they did was wrong!" Yes, there are a few who unfortunately have been wrongly convicted of crimes they did not commit. Should anyone listen to these stories long enough and accept them as factual, one would think that all of them have been wrongly convicted. They were framed! They were set up! They didn't do it! Needless to say the vast majority are in prison because of crimes they committed. No one else is to blame.

My story telling wasn't any different than theirs. I shirked full responsibility and freely disbursed blame anywhere I could "logically" place it. A day finally came when my own guilt and remorse seized me like never before. One day as I was retelling my arrest encounter to another inmate, it hit me. I was playing the "Blame Game". I had played it so often that I was almost believing it. That's a dangerous place to be. Recidivism breeds in this kind of climate. I finished telling him my story (blaming others) and went back to my cell for the night. That night was a restless night. God was dealing with my heart and I was dealing with the truth. Shifting blame not only negates full responsibility but it perpetuates the lie. By not taking full responsibility for our actions we are lying to ourselves and lying to God. I was lying to God. That's serious stuff. It will not fly in the face of truth.

My time finally arrived. I made a conscious decision that night to get my story straight. It wouldn't be easy. I had told the "Blame Game" version of my story so many times that it was second nature to me. If I wasn't careful it could happen again. I determined in my heart to take full responsibility. Like my mom would suggest to me, I had decided to "Say it like I meant it." So I did. Without minimizing my sin and a trending willingness to be blaming other circumstances, I confessed what I felt was my greatest of all sins to God. I shot my neighbor! He died! I did it! The writing of this encounter is in part also to set the record straight of a most remorseful and heavy heart. The man in my mirror was fully to blame. Later on that evening as I was acknowledging and confessing anew the sin of greatest severity in my life genuine remorse began taking up residence in my heart like never before. It was a painful and emotional encounter with the truth yet it freed me to enter another level of maturity. Repentance of my crime (sin) felt more thorough and complete. My court conviction finally gave way to the conviction of the Holy Spirit. It was a necessary part of my Christian journey. God is always calling us to higher ground. He is always transforming us into his image. *"And we, who with unveiled faces all reflect the Lord's glory, are being transformed into his likeness with ever-increasing glory, which comes from the Lord, who is the Spirit." (2Corinthians 3:18)* The "Blame Game" had finally ended. I surrendered to the truth. In the end, the truth always wins.

# Chapter Twenty-Two

## A Time of Testing

*"Testing will surely come."*
*(Ezekiel 21:13a)*

When I first entered Attica Prison I had ten years in front of me. A ten-year sentence does not necessarily mean you would have to serve the full ten years. Time off for good behavior was an inmate's best friend. It was the incentive that restrained many and greatly aided in keeping calm within the prison. By keeping my nose clean and not causing the C.O.s any problems, I could possibly see a reduction of my sentence. I was determined to gain as much good time as possible. Within the first two and a half years my good behavior was again producing benefit in my life and by early 1979 I was transferred out of Attica's notorious B-Block and into my new home in Attica's Honor Block. Admittance into Honor Block wasn't easy. Only the best inmates would be accepted.

Attica housed over 2,200 inmates in cells that were built in 1931. It's old and it's dank. The gray walls and poor lighting greatly contributed to the depressing surroundings, but the Honor Block which housed approximately 50 inmates was different. The newer cells were bigger and brighter, both hot and cold running water were available for each inmate, and a huge day-room with a café-style atmosphere was available for use. It might not seem like much, but it was hugely different. I always considered living in the Honor Block to be both a personal achievement and a gift of God's favor upon my life. *"Whoever disregards discipline comes to poverty and shame, but whoever heeds correction is honored". (Proverbs 13:18)* Although it was still a way off, I was one step closer to the goal of most every inmate, a parole date. Six months passed. It was now March-April of 1979 and my time had finally arrived to meet with the Minimum Period of Incarceration Board. (MPI Board) This board would evaluate me and determine my earliest possible release date.

It was impossible to know how much time you had left in front of you until you'd met with this board. I recall the board consisting of four to five people, each one asking a series of questions designed to help them determine my MPI. Our meeting lasted about 20 minutes.......20 long grueling minutes. No determination would be made that day. I extended a cordial thank you to the Board and headed back to my cell. For the next couple days there was only one thing on my mind, the board's decision. Three long days passed and there it was. A note from the MPI Board was placed on my bars by one of the officers. "Good Luck," he said as he walked away. With note in hand I prayed and asked the Lord for a favorable decision.

Thirty minutes later I was still clutching the unopened note as faith and fear were waging a battle in my mind. The voice of faith within me declared, "Go ahead and open it! God's Favor is upon you." Yet in sharp contrast, fear raised its voice shouting back, "Disappointment will come." I was determined to open the note in faith not fear. The board had the authority to set my minimum as little as four years or give me the maximum of ten years. It was their prerogative yet it was God's will for my life that would prevail. Faith was rising up inside of me. It was time to open the note. I prayed and I opened it. There it was. That lovely number "4". My minimum time was now set at four years. With almost three years behind me, my release date could possibly be a little over one year away. Praise the

Lord. According to many Bible scholars the number "4" in Scripture represents "a time testing". God does not tempt us but He does test us. Could it be that God was saying to me that these four years represented a time of testing? *"Because you know that the testing of your faith produces perseverance. (James 1:3) and "……having stood the test, that person will receive the crown of life that the Lord has promised to those who love Him." (James 1:12b)* Another step closer!

Soon I'd be leaving the maximum security of Attica Prison to serve my remaining sentence in Albion Prison, a medium security facility about one hour (50 miles) due north of Attica. I applied for transfer and was accepted. In May 1979, wearing handcuffs and shackles, I left the gray walls of Attica behind. God had been so very good to me. His promised protection and peaceful presence were my constant companions. Attica didn't leave any scars of incarceration upon my life, but I left my mark on it. I was not only leaving Attica Prison, I was leaving my church. The fellowship of believers is a strong bond that isn't easily broken. My joy of leaving was slightly dampened with the sadness of saying good-bye to my brothers in Christ. With a strong church behind me I headed out.

Whenever someone left the prison, we'd always tell them, "Don't look back." and I was told the same. But as we drove away I couldn't resist peering out of the van window to look back at the prison where so much had happened. The wall didn't seem as imposing as it did nearly three years before. The church was alive and well behind the wall of Attica Prison. Etched in my memory were many encounters from behind that wall. Faces I would never forget and experiences that are a constant reminder of God's faithfulness. I was saying good-bye to brothers who I will one day see again when we will all meet in our home in heaven.

# *Twice Convicted*

*"Continue to remember those in prison as if you were together with them, and those who are mistreated as if you yourselves were suffering." (Hebrews 13:3)* The van arrived at Albion Correctional Facility as I began my final descent from prison life.

# Chapter Twenty-Three

## Not all pilots fly planes

*"See, I am doing a new thing! Now it springs up; do you not perceive it? I am making a way in the wilderness and streams in the wasteland."*
*(Isaiah 43:19 NIV)*

It didn't take me very long to become settled in at Albion. No gun towers lurking over us, no tear gas canisters waiting to be released in the mess hall, far less tension, and much more freedom. The forty-foot wall that I viewed daily in Attica was no longer before my eyes. The barbed wire fence around the perimeter of my new environment was more than adequate in hindering escapes. The thought of being sent back to the "Big House" (Attica) was sufficient reason for preventing escapes. Serious disciplinary problems were few and those who violated the rules were quickly sent back behind the wall.

Today Albion is an exclusively female prison but in the late 1970's it was a co-ed facility with men and women housed in separate barracks that were strictly off limits to each other. Physical contact with women inmates was absolutely forbidden, and violators, if caught, soon found themselves wearing leg shackles and handcuffs, and given a free bus ride back to a maximum security facility. *"Watch and pray that you will not fall into temptation; the spirit is willing but the flesh is weak." (Matthew 26:41)* Inmates understood the penalty for inappropriate contact with the opposite sex, yet these encounters did sometimes occur.

The growing female inmate population as well as the need to eliminate these physical encounters eventually led to Albion becoming an exclusively female prison by 1986.

Within a few weeks (June-July 1979) I was given my new assignment, Chaplain's Inmate Assistant. It was primarily an administrative position helping the Chaplain with filing, typing, and running errands. I considered it a great privilege working alongside this man of God. Little did I know then, but God was indeed preparing me for things to come. The church at Albion was uniquely different. It was a healthy church but it was also a church made up primarily of short timers awaiting their release. Most of the church attendees were far less involved in church activities because of work release assignments, family visits, and occasional week-end passes that were granted to those who met the requirements. Unlike Attica, which had a strong united body of believers, the church in Albion was much more of a road side chapel with both men and women inmates constantly arriving and leaving the facility.

The summer of 1979 seemed to go by very slowly. As most inmates did in Albion, I applied for a work release program and was waiting to hear from the committee that would determine my eligibility. Those who were accepted into this program were allowed to work outside the prison in local factories, warehouses, nursing homes, etc. Money earned from these jobs equipped inmates with finances they could use upon release. Although most jobs paid the minimum wage it was far better than the few dollars earned through prison work assignments. As I recall, being the chaplain's assistant I earned about $12 per week. In early August my opportunity to meet with the state work release board had finally arrived. Little did I know it at the time, but I was in for a big surprise.

# *Not all Pilots Fly Planes*

I nervously sat before the members of the work release committee as they introduced themselves to me. Unlike other committees they were rather pleasant. They carefully reviewed my folder and politely questioned me about my past, present, and future ambitions. Their determination regarding my eligibility for work release was an important decision. Was I a high risk to society or would they consider me a safe prospect for work release into the community? Their evaluation would determine my future. I was seeking their approval for the work release program but God had other things in mind. God was grooming me for something else; my call into ministry.

About 20 minutes into our meeting the chairperson of the committee looked squarely into my eyes and asked me the question that set the course for my remaining time. "Have you considered a school release program?" "School release program," I asked, "What's that? I never heard of a school release program!" They proceeded to explain.

For a number of years the New York State Department of Corrections had been considering piloting an education program to help inmates upon their release into society. Albion Correctional Facility would be first to test such a program. Contingent upon acceptance into an area college, eligible inmates would be allowed to leave the prison every morning and return each evening after school. It worked much like the work release program. The only difference being inmates would be in a classroom rather than at a work site. They wanted me to be the test pilot of this new program. The future of the program would rest heavily upon my shoulders. If successful, other inmates might travel down the same road; if unsuccessful, that would be the end of it. After reviewing my folder, the committee felt that I was their best prospect for a successful launching. "Think it over for a few days; work release or the school release program." The decision was actually mine. I had one week to decide.

Decisions, decisions, decisions! I had it all planned out to save as much money as I could prior to being released. Now I faced a decision that would greatly change what I thought were the plans of my heart. *"In their hearts humans plan their course, but the Lord establishes their steps." (Proverbs 16:19)* I only had a week to determine what I believed to be God's will for my life. I earnestly prayed for clarity and God answered my prayer. Within a few days I received a completely unexpected visit from Don, a Christian friend I knew who lived in North Chili, New York. North Chili is a small town about 30 miles east of the prison. It's also where Roberts Wesleyan Christian College is located. As I began to tell him about my dilemma he immediately chimed in, "Now I know why the Lord wanted me to visit you today." He was a personal friend of the Dean of Roberts Wesleyan College and for the next few hours proceeded to tell me all about the school and the courses they offered. The more he talked, the more excited I became. The more excited I became, the more convinced I was that God was opening the door for me to attend. Our visit ended and my decision was made. If at all possible I was going to attend a Christian College at the expense of the New York State Department of Corrections and a special scholarship program offered by Roberts Wesleyan College.

A few hurdles however, still remained. *"With man this is impossible, but with God all things are possible." (Matthew 19:26)* A few more days passed and I received another unexpected visit. I didn't see any familiar faces as I entered the visiting room. As I stood there wondering who had come to visit me, I noticed two well-dressed distinguished-looking men motioning me to come and sit at their table. As I sat down they introduced themselves as the

President and the Dean of Student Admissions of Roberts Wesleyan. They had a very important decision to make; should I be admitted into their college? They asked some very pointed questions about my conviction. Their concerns were many and well justified. How would a convicted felon fit into their campus? What would be the reaction of the trustees and the Board of Directors? Would parents remove their children from the school? How would I be received by other students? What would the professors say? Would I instill fear into a normally tranquil college campus? Their ultimate decision, if wrong, could bring scandal to an otherwise highly respected college. They had so little to gain, so much to lose; but God was in control of my destiny.

Our meeting ended with a hearty hand shake and the words, "I'm sure you'll enjoy attending Roberts Wesleyan College." A few days later, I sat before the release committee with my acceptance letter in hand. By early September 1979 I was enrolled in college-level Bible courses in a Christian College. God was indeed directing my life! *"....being confident of this, that he who began a good work in you will carry it on to completion until the day of Christ Jesus." (Philippians 1:6)* I was the pilot of this new program and I was determined not to disappoint the state, myself, and most importantly, God.

# Chapter Twenty-Four

## Blowing in the Wind

*"........stormy winds that do His bidding"*
*(Psalm 148:8b)*

As you might imagine, living at the prison while attending a college outside was very busy and demanding. My Monday–Friday schedule pushed me to near exhaustion on a daily basis, but I loved every minute of it. Other than being paroled, what else could an inmate ask for? I was free from the prison almost 14 hours every day. A glimpse of my daily schedule reveals my tight, busy routine

| | |
|---|---|
| Wake-up call | 4:15 am |
| Breakfast in the prison | 4:45 am |
| Out-take processing | 5:15 am |
| Board prison shuttle bus | 5:45 am |
| Arrive downtown Rochester | 6:45 am |
| Board public transportation | 7:15 am |
| Arrive at the college | 8:15 am |
| First class starting | 9:00 am |
| Last class ending | 4:00 pm |
| Reverse the process | 4:30 pm |
| Arrive back in Albion Prison | 7:30 pm |

By the time I ate dinner, studied a few hours, and eventually hit the shower it was 11 pm. The minute my head hit the pillow I was out for the night. By Friday evening I was both physically and mentally exhausted. "Thank God it's Friday" (T.G.I.F.) rapidly became my favorite expression. With the exception of end of term breaks and vacation days, my grueling schedule for the next nine months typically remained the same.......except for one day, one day quite different from all the rest.

In order to prevent escapes by those not approved for release programs the morning out-take procedure had to be very precise. Before leaving the prison grounds careful attention was given to each inmate to ensure who they were and that they were properly cleared for work release. (In my case, school release). Inmates could withdraw a few dollars from their account to assist them with daily needs, such as bus fare, meals, cigarettes etc. Five to ten dollars was usually more than enough for each day. Special permission had to be granted for larger withdrawals. Receipts for all inmate expenditures were expected upon returning each evening to thwart the purchase of drugs, alcohol, and other contraband. Every inmate understood that random urine tests were taken and if you were found with dirty urine (drugs or alcohol in your system) you could kiss Albion good-bye and say "Hello" again to Attica Prison.

Larger amounts of money could be withdrawn if an inmate could prove his request was warranted. Of course these requests would be scrutinized by the administration for approval. Frivolous requests were quickly denied. Legitimate ones were generally granted. I submitted one such request for additional educational costs (campus mail-box fees) of $35. Including my normal withdrawal for meals and bus fare, my request totaled $75 for the week. My request was deemed reasonable and approved. At the end of that week (Friday) I would be expected to show a receipt for my additional expense. I arrived on campus Monday morning with an extra $35 in my wallet and every intention of paying my mail box fee that week.

# *Blowing in the Wind*

Monday was a very busy day and I wasn't able to see the school's finance department to make payment. No problem, I had all week to accomplish this little task. I decided that instead of carrying the money in my wallet and taking the chance of losing it I would put it in a safe place, my campus mailbox. On Tuesday afternoon, as I was studying in the school library, a student from one of my classes sat next to me and began talking about a dilemma she was facing. She wanted to travel to her hometown near Albany, New York for an important family matter but didn't have the finances to get there. She knew I was an inmate on a school release program and didn't expect me to have any way of financially helping her; she just needed someone to talk with. If she could borrow the money from someone on campus she would immediately leave for home and return back for class the next day. She said her parents had money for her and she'd be able to repay the loan upon her return on Wednesday. As I listened to her the thought came to me that maybe I could help. I had the money to help her out as long as she could assure me I'd have it back in my hand the next day or Friday at the latest. "How much do you need?" I asked. She told me $25-$30 would be more than enough to meet her needs.

I never should have said it, but I said, "Come with me. I think I can help you out." We walked across campus to the mail room and I opened my mail box. I handed her $35 and said "It's a short-term loan and you must be sure to get it back in my hands by Friday." She assured me that it would not be a problem. I became very concerned when I didn't see her on campus for the next couple of days. Before heading back to the prison that evening I checked my mail-box and found a note in it. Apparently on Thursday afternoon she called the mailroom clerk and asked him to leave a message from her in my mailbox. It simply read, "Sorry I won't be back until Monday, crisis in the family."

Apparently she failed to understand the crisis of my own that I would be facing on Friday, one that could jeopardize my parole and send me back to Attica. How could something that seemed so right be turning out so wrong? *"There is a way that appears to be right, but in the end it leads to death." (Proverbs 14:12)* Now time was running out on me and fear was gripping my heart. On my way back to the prison that evening I couldn't help but think about the problem I'd be facing the next day. That night I prayed and placed the situation entirely into God's hands. Although my problem was serious God still had everything under control.

I woke up Friday morning went through the normal out-processing and headed out to school. As usual, the prison shuttle dropped me off at the bus stop in downtown Rochester and I waited for my bus. It arrived on schedule. I greeted the bus driver, paid my fare, and off it went. I noticed that we had a different driver that day. As usual, I found a seat and opened a book. I routinely used my hourly commute to study and catch up on my reading assignments. The bus continued its route picking up and dropping off its passengers. As I occasionally glanced up to see who was boarding I noticed something strangely different. Not only was the bus driver different, the passengers were not the ones I was used to seeing each day. Not thinking much about it, I put my face back into my book. About 45 minutes later the bus stopped in front of a large factory and all the remaining passengers disembarked. As I sat there the bus driver said, "OK buddy, it's time to get off. This is the end of the line." What was he talking about? What's going on? Where am I? I picked up my books and headed to the front of the bus. "I thought we were headed to North Chili. Where are we?" At that the driver said, "You boarded the wrong bus if you wanted to go there. We are at the Eastman-Kodak Plant. I'll be resting here for a few minutes and then turning around and heading back downtown." I said I was sure that the banner on the front of the bus read it was going to North Chili and not Eastman-Kodak. At that he said, "I apologize for the confusion. You're right, it did read North Chili. I forgot to change the bus banner until after you boarded I'm sorry for the inconvenience but you'll have to get off." "How far are we from North Chili?" I asked. He said it was a good 15 miles away. I couldn't believe what I was hearing. I boarded the wrong bus and was miles away from school. The corrections department made it very clear; I was to travel directly to school and directly back. Any deviation from that routine would not be tolerated. How would I explain this? After six months of getting on the right bus there was no acceptable excuse for getting on the wrong one. Coupled with my $35 dilemma, I was sure I'd be heading back to Attica.

The bus driver gave me directions to Roberts Wesleyan College. I stepped off the bus and headed down the road. It was too far to walk and it also wasn't on a bus route. My only choice was to hitch-hike. "Lord, I need your help" I inwardly cried, and started walking backwards with my thumb out in desperate need of a ride. It was about 8 o'clock, I was 15 miles from school, and my class was to start in about an hour. My professors at the college were clearly instructed to immediately report any tardiness or absenteeism to the prison officials. I continued walking backwards as car after car, truck after truck passed me. A New York State trooper even passed me by. (Whew, that was really close) It was almost 8:30 and I was still a long way from my destination. How could I have been as foolish as to loan out $35? Why didn't I pay attention to the bus I was boarding? My hopes of gaining an early parole date were quickly fading away. I continued walking backwards, with my thumb out, as I privately held my one-man pity party.

# *Twice Convicted*

As I walked, the wind started blowing. March in western New York is windy and dirty. Most of the seasonal snow had melted away, leaving behind the accumulation of several months of dirt and debris. In a few more weeks the street sweepers would be attacking the problem, but until then the highways remained a mess. Add the March winds to the dirt and debris, and you end up with terrible walking conditions. My eyes were irritated, my nose was running, and the wind kept its blustery force upon me. The wind howled at times and occasionally formed small whirl winds that traveled down the road. Several times I had to stop and clear my eyes and wipe my nose as I continued my trek along this wind-swept highway.

Another whirlwind started heading my way and when it reached me it brought with it an accumulation of dirt, debris, old newspaper pages and other flying debris. The wind temporally abated leaving dirt and trash on me. I shook off the filth and removed a piece of newspaper wrapped across my chest. After wiping my face and clearing my nose, I removed one final piece of paper from off my leg. It was an envelope; a fairly new and unopened envelope. There wasn't any identification written on it and I could feel there was something inside. I opened it and found $35. I couldn't believe my eyes. I looked around to see if someone was walking by that may have dropped it but there wasn't a soul in sight. The lyrics to a 1960's song by Bob Dylan declared, "*The answer my friend, is blowing in the wind.*" The answer to my financial problem was solved. Was it a coincidence? I doubt it. Was it my lucky day? I don't buy that theory either. Someone lost it, possibly, but I don't think so. The amount was $35, exactly what I needed. The money was even in crisp uncirculated-looking currency. I can't explain miracles, but I know they happen, and this one happened to me. "*........stormy winds that do His bidding". (Psalm 148:8b)* The dictionary defines a "miracle" as an extraordinary event manifesting Divine intervention in human affairs. To that one I say AMEN.

My countenance changed like that of a chameleon. My heavy heart gave way to joy and I trust my whole countenance must have telegraphed a different hitch-hiker. With my thumb out again, almost immediately a semi-truck stopped and I got in. "Where you headed?" he asked. "I'm headed to Roberts Wesleyan College in North Chili." I responded. With that he said "This must be your lucky day! I'm traveling right past the place." I thanked him for picking me up, but I knew it was so much more than my lucky day. It was a blessing from the Lord, the favor of God. The driver dropped me off on Route 33, Buffalo Road, right at the entrance of the college. I ran across the athletic field, hurried into my class room in Hastings Hall and sat down at my desk, not a minute too soon. The 9 o'clock bell rang for class and I was sitting there, right where I was supposed to be (probably with a smirk on my face). Before heading back to the prison that day, my mail box fee was paid and I had my receipt in hand. For fear of the administration finding out that I loaned $35 to a classmate, I had to keep my miracle experience a secret. It wasn't until after my release from prison that I felt it was time to share the miracle story. *"You are the God who performs miracles..." (Psalm 77:14a)*

# Chapter Twenty-Five

## Prisoner of Hope

*"Set me free from my prison, that I may praise your name." (Psalm 142:7)*

I waited patiently for almost four years and my date with the parole board had finally arrived. I was notified that my board hearing was set for sometime in late April, only a few weeks away. The parole board had a notorious reputation of being totally unpredictable and their decision was final. If they approved your parole, you could be released within a few weeks. If not, you could remain incarcerated for a year or longer without any avenue for appeal. A number of things would be factored into their decision; including time served, victim impact statements, judicial recommendations, remorse, prison behavior, and criminal history to name a few. I also believe that an inmate's demeanor when appearing before the board can significantly affect their decision. Manners and respect do make a difference!

Needless to say, I was very nervous as I walked in and sat down at the table before them. I don't remember exactly how many members were on the panel that day, possibly five or six, but it seemed as if a hundred eyes were fixed on me. The next 30 minutes would seem to be the longest minutes of my life. They asked a wide variety of questions about my past, my present, and what I planned to do with my life if I were to be paroled. I wanted to display confidence not arrogance, humility not pretentiousness. If I attempted to oversell myself I was sure they would have the ability to see right through any facade. I had to be real, and the real me was a "Born Again Christian". Would the Parole Board believe that? Over the years many had attempted to "sell" their Christianity to the board to no avail. Jail-house converts seldom impressed them. I had a dilemma. Give God the glory or take personal credit for the changes that God worked into in my life.

"After reviewing your record, we see you've worked hard to turn your life around. You don't appear to be the same person you were over four years ago." I wondered had I gained the respect of corrections officers and the administration? Uncommon to most inmates, I didn't have any disciplinary action against me during my entire incarceration. My record was clean. I could have easily embraced the compliments of the Parole Board yet I knew the accomplishments were the result of God's hand upon my life. All I had to offer Him was my broken life, a convicted felon. In exchange, He offered me a future. *"He chose the lowly things of this world and the despised things....and the things that are not....to nullify the things that are, so that no one may boast before Him". (1Corinthians 1:28-29)*

*A*lthough I appreciated the kind words, I could not quietly sit back and receive their kudos. Gaining accolades for the achievements which belong to another is wrong. At the risk of changing what appeared to be a favorable atmosphere I felt compelled to say, "Thank you for such kind words. I appreciate them, but I want you to know that it was Jesus Christ who changed my life. He deserves the credit." The chairperson responded, "Whatever! All we know is that you worked hard and we can see the change."

"Thank you very much Mr. Cebula. You will receive a notification of our decision in two weeks." TWO WEEKS! That is an eternity! I would have to wait 14 days in mental anguish. That's 1,206,600 seconds. Tick.....tick.....tick, the seconds passed by until every one of them was used up and the day of decision had finally arrived. A corrections officer visited me with the sealed letter in his hand. "Good Luck, Phil! I hope you make it." Before opening it, I reminded myself of all the prayers concerning this very moment that had been offered up on my behalf. I waited four years for this decision. Why was I stalling? It was time to open it. I offered a final prayer, and with trepidation opened the letter. **PAROLE GRANTED**. My release date was set for late May 1980. I would soon leave my prison life behind. For four years I lived in hope of this day's arrival. I was returning home, but things would be so very different. I wasn't the same person I used to be. I believed God had plans for my life but I was still in the dark as to what those plans were. *"Return to your fortress, you prisoners of hope; even now I announce that I will restore twice as much to you. (Zechariah 9:12)* His promise for my future gave me assurance that my future looked bright. He will lead the way. *'I have decided to follow Jesus. No turning back! No turning back!'*

# Chapter Twenty-Six

## A New Lease on Life

*"I have much to write to you, but I do not want to use paper and ink. Instead, I hope to visit you and talk with you face to face, so that our joy may be complete."*
*(2nd John 1:12)*

**R**e-adjusting to life outside of prison would be an ongoing challenge. Upon my return to the western New York area I found myself searching for purpose in life. Was God calling me into the ministry? Would a convicted felon be accepted or rejected by the church community? Would my divorce hinder God's plan for my life? I moved from one location to another, attempting to fit in yet not knowing where. I attended one church after another in search of the place God wanted me to be. The next two years would be a time of testing for me. I worked in various jobs and while I would abstain completely from drugs and alcohol, I failed to abstain from a few relationships. During this period I found myself in an arena of temptation, battling with loneliness and strong desire for companionship. Never did I walk away from my faith, but there were numerous times when the light of Christ within me was barely luminous. My walk with God was far from perfect. Although I continued to witness for the Lord when presented with the opportunity, I had fallen into a lapse where I did want it His way but I also wanted it my way. While my conscience had become somewhat hardened, there always lingered within me a sense of guilt over what I knew was my tarnished lifestyle. This struggle continued for almost two years. Then one day I received a phone call that would forever change the course of my life.

# Twice Convicted

*"I was pushed back and about to fall, but the Lord helped me." (Psalm 118:13*

I picked up the phone and I heard, "Hi Phil! How's it going?" The voice sounded familiar but I couldn't place it. "Who is this?" I questioned. "It's Mike, Mike Kropman". I could hardly believe what I heard. Mike and I were best friends in Attica Prison. We went our separate ways in the late 70's and I never thought I'd hear from him again. Mike was (is) evangelism personified. Together we made quite a team. His zeal for God was always exuberant and contagious. We prayed together, witnessed together, studied together, and even sang together. We were novice guitarists but it didn't stop us from leading praise and worship when we had the opportunity. Our personalities were as different as night and day, yet we blended together making our mark in the dark places of the prison.

"Where are you Mike? What's happening?" He proceeded to tell me how he moved from New York State (Rochester area) to Woonsocket, Rhode Island. "What in the world are you doing in Woonsocket?" He proceeded to tell me how he kept in contact with our former Attica Prison Chaplain Rev. Normand Farrington who had moved to Rhode Island and was now the pastor of a church in downtown Woonsocket. Pastor Farrington was our "father in the faith". He mentored us for several years, making a great impact upon our lives. Mike was now attending his church and was in the process of becoming the assistant Pastor. "When are you coming down?" he queried. "I know Pastor Farrington would love to see you, and so would I. Pray about it and get back to me." Mike's invitation had struck a chord within my heart as I thought about the possibilities of serving the Lord alongside Pastor Farrington and his newly appointed assistant Michael Kropman. To accomplish anything like this would take another miracle.

At that time I was still under the supervision of the New York State department of parole with many restrictions on my life, one of which was not leaving the state without good reason and the authority of my parole officer (P.O.). Just visiting Rhode Island would take a small miracle. Moving to Woonsocket to be with another felon would take a major miracle. After a couple days of prayer I called my P.O. and set up a meeting to request permission for an out-of-state visit. It's not often that a parolee calls his parole officer. It's usually the other way around. "You called me Phil, what do you want?" he said with authority. "I'd like to visit Woonsocket, Rhode Island." I proceeded to explain my relationship with Pastor Farrington and how much he meant to me. I purposely avoided talking about Mike, a convicted felon. I knew if I mentioned him it would greatly hinder my chance of going. My request was granted and I was approved for the last two weeks of August with instructions to call him upon arrival and again upon my return.

# Chapter Twenty-Seven

## Compelling Reason

*"And now, compelled by the Spirit, I am going to Jerusalem, not knowing what will happen to me there." (Acts 20:22)*

I called Mike and Pastor Farrington and gave them the dates of my upcoming visit. My 1972 Triumph motorcycle was my choice of transportation to Rhode Island. The bike was purring like a kitten as I traveled down the highway. My goal was to arrive before sunset. As I neared Hartford, Connecticut my trusty Triumph suddenly began to lose power. Fifty miles short of my destination of Woonsocket the engine died. I almost made it! It was 8pm.

I found a nearby phone booth and upon calling Mike I said, "Help, I'm stranded in Hartford!" I gave him my location and he said he'd get his pick-up truck and come and rescue me. Was this really God's will for me to be here? Should I have stayed at home? Several hours passed and Mike finally arrived at 11pm. We loaded my motorcycle onto the back of his truck and off we went. Woonsocket, here I come.

It was great seeing Pastor Farrington and Mike again. We spent hours catching up on each other's lives. Mike was married to Linda and raising a family. Reverend Farrington was pastor of the Woonsocket church, and together with his lovely wife Marion they were impacting the city. The church was an older building, a beautiful edifice in the downtown area but it was not the church God had shown me in my mind's eye. Mike always made me feel very welcomed in the area as he introduced me to as many people as he could. "You should move here", he would repeatedly say. "It's a great place for ministry. God is really moving in our church!" Although my heart was confirming what Mike was saying, I kept it to myself. I wasn't quite ready to affirm his assertion and jump into anything too rapidly. God was teaching me not to be so quick to respond to everything presented to me. At times my impulsive behavior left behind regrets and I was determined for history not to repeat itself.

Sunday morning service was fantastic. The presence of God filled the sanctuary, coupled with responsive worship and a warm and friendly congregation. When the altar call was given several people came forward and received Jesus Christ into their heart. The only disappointing moment was when Pastor Farrington dismissed the congregation with his benediction. I could have stayed in church all day. Sunday evening service was the same, and again several people came forward to receive Christ. Later that evening Mike acknowledged that people were getting saved at almost every service. God was moving, the church was growing, and lives were being changed. Who could ask for anything more? What a wonderful place to be!

A couple home Bible studies, mid week services and another Sunday were passing by too fast. My two-week visit was rapidly coming to an end and soon I would be headed back to Western New York. Since my motorcycle was still out of commission Mike offered to let me borrow his car for my trip home. I now had two reasons for returning to Woonsocket; one, I had to return his car, and two, my motorcycle still needed repair. Was there a third reason? Was God indeed calling me there? Was this God's way of seeing to it that I returned? As I made my plans to journey back to New York State, Mike's words played over and over in my mind, "Phil, maybe you should move here." Was Mike right? All the way back home I pondered his statement and by the time I pulled into my driveway I knew the answer. Yes, God indeed was calling me to New England! Now if I could just convince my Parole Officer to release me.

Upon my return to New York I called my P.O. and arranged another visit with him. As we sat in my kitchen, with his rather firm voice he repeated the words of his last visit. "You called me Phil, what do you want?" I got right to the point and said, "I'm requesting permission to move to Rhode Island. I believe that God has a plan for my life and moving there is a part of that plan." He stared at me for a few moments then broke his silence and said, "It's possible but not probable. Even if I'm willing to approve it, I am not your biggest obstacle. Unless you have a very compelling reason such as your family living there, it is highly unlikely to happen." He went on to explain that I was a ward of the state of New York and they were responsible for the supervision of my life until my parole was completed. "Releasing you would be the easy part. Rhode Island must agree to add you to their books and they have more than enough of their own parolees to worry about. Here's what I'll do for you; I'll grant you another two-week pass during which time you will have to arrange a meeting with the Rhode Island Department of Parole and explain to them what your desires and goals are. If they will accept you, I'll release you. Good Luck!" I accepted his "Good Luck" proclamation and began making plans for my second trip to Rhode Island.

# Chapter Twenty-Eight

## That Didn't Take Long

*"The lot is cast into the lap,*
*but its every decision is from the Lord.*
*(Proverbs 16:33)*

My meeting with the Rhode Island Parole supervisor had finally arrived. "Mr. Cebula, the supervisor will now see you." I had come this far by faith and I was determined to continue walking in that faith! I sat down in a chair that seemed to be two sizes too big for me. Lost in this huge chair I wondered if this was the department's way of reminding parolees that the man behind the desk had the authority and we were just the little people. "How may I help you?" was the simple question from behind the desk. With that I proceeded to explain my reasons for requesting a parole transfer from New York State. He listened intently as I talked about my born-again experience. I believe the Holy Spirit was leading my answers as he continued asking more questions. His penetrating curiosity emboldened me to the point where I found myself planting little seeds of God's Word into our discourse. I was tempted to ask him if he wanted to ask the Lord into his heart, but I rejected the prompt. I did hope that I was planting seeds that others would someday water. *"I planted the seed, Apollos watered it, but God has been making it grow" (1Corinthians 3:6)*

I didn't have to wait very long for his decision. I had expected the answer to my request to take several weeks or longer, so I was awestruck when his decision was made that day. After 30 minutes of sharing my testimony and reasons for wanting to live there he declared, "OK, we will make the necessary arrangements for your transfer. I will notify your Parole Officer in New York State to corroborate your story, and if he does indeed approve, our departments will expedite all the necessary paperwork to finalize the transaction. Welcome to the Ocean State! Don't disappoint us." I said thank you and reassured him that I had every intention of keeping on the straight and narrow. We shook hands and I walked out of his office. I think I was walking on cloud nine as the favor of the Lord was again upon me. "Thank you Lord!"

It took me almost a full month to make all the necessary arrangements for the move and by mid September 1982 I was living in Woonsocket. I would miss my family and friends back in New York, but for the next few years this would be my home. Within a few weeks Pastor Farrington was using me in small ways at the church. Everything was falling into place. The only thing that seemed to be missing in my life was a wife. My heart's desire was to find someone, get settled down, and raise a family. Irene was a new Christian and was faithfully attending church. She claims to have spotted me first, and by November of 1982 we were dating. Irene and her beautiful two-year-old daughter Jennifer were rapidly making an impression on my life. It didn't take very long for us to fall in love and on the evening of April 3rd 1983 Irene and I were married.

Our family soon began growing and on January 9, 1984 our son Daniel Philip was born. Four months later on May 21, 1984, adoption proceedings were finalized and Jennifer Lynn was officially my (our) daughter. Although our daughter Andrea, from my earlier marriage was living over 450 miles away in Buffalo, New York, we kept in constant communication with her and visited as often as we could. Her mother Karen was doing a superb job in raising her to be a fine young lady. Irene's love for Andrea was immediate and motherly, and she has always embraced her as her own. She is most certainly a part of our family. With one more daughter yet to be born, we were on the road to discover our destiny.

My days became filled with increased demands, between juggling family time, church life, and a forty-plus hour job. My participation in church activities continued to increase as I joined the worship team, taught the new believers Sunday school class, became a board member, and also hosted and taught a weekly home Bible study group. Pastor Farrington occasionally would ask me to preach at the church and also invited me to be a part of monthly clergy meetings with Northern Rhode Island area pastors. I was in the process of realizing God's will for my life and I loved every minute of it. If Pastor Farrington had a revelation concerning my future he wasn't telling me, yet I wondered if he was mentoring me for something else.

# Chapter Twenty-Nine

## Quest for Guidance

*"Let the wise learn and add to their learning, and let the discerning get guidance." (Proverbs 1:5)*

By the summer of 1984 I was deeply involved in the life of our church. Although I felt secure in my job, I was beginning to sense my future could be somewhere else. Countless times people would say, "Phil, you have a call on your life! Don't you think God is calling you to pastor a church?" One day as I sat at one of the area clergy meetings I felt deeply uncomfortable about my lack of knowing if God indeed had a greater call on my life. Others were suggesting it as well and I desperately wanted it to be true. During my incarceration in Attica I had plenty of indicators of a possible call into the ministry.

I wondered if it was God calling me to be a pastor of a church or was it simply my own desire. I began asking other pastors about their confirmation call and much to my surprise no two stories were alike. Some were called in their early years, others later in life. Some heard the call while going through personal crisis, while others heard the voice of God after achieving high levels of personal success. I remember talking to a prominent pediatrician who laid down his medical practice after hearing from the Lord, to follow the call of God into the mission field. All of their stories were riveting testimonies yet none of them were identical. The only thing consistent was they all were absolutely convinced that the Lord had called them into service for Him. I craved that same strong confirmation for myself.

# *Twice Convicted*

My wife Irene and I discussed it often. A more supportive wife I could not have found. Even though she sensed the frustration I was having, she patiently waited with me. We prayed together; no answer. We fasted together; no answer. We talked about stepping out in faith to discover God's will in this. Irene would repeatedly say to me, "Honey, you need to get away by yourself. Take a few days off from work and spend time with God. Maybe then God would clarify things for us." She was right and I took her up on the offer.

On a Friday morning in the middle of June, I packed a few things into my 1972 American Motors Gremlin and headed down the highway searching for an answer. I wasn't sure where to go, so I headed west until I entered into Connecticut. As I continued on I finally saw a rural dirt road. After a few miles and the dirt road becoming more rural, I eventually turned onto what would have been akin to an old logging trail. Finally coming to a fallen tree, this was the end of the line. I felt it was the perfect place. I had brought plenty of water but no food as I began to pray and fast and wait; asking God to speak to me. I was determined not to leave until I knew. Was God calling me to be a pastor or not?

**Actual Car & Site**

The weather was summer perfect, the mosquitoes minimal, and the environment serene. The only sounds were the sounds of the forest, leaves rustling, birds chirping, and small critters scurrying across the field. I took out my guitar and began to worship God in song. Soon His presence filled the wilderness sanctuary wherein I sat. I petitioned for His WORD that would speak directly into my heart concerning my particular situation. God has a way of speaking directly into one's life; that's what I needed.

Friday evening came and went without such a WORD. I awoke early Saturday morning to the penetrating sun heating up the inside of the car. Saturday was much like Friday, reading my Bible, praying, singing, and waiting. The result was again the same. No WORD. As I lay there that evening I began to question the reasonableness of my demands. I was demanding God to speak to me with full expectation. Was I acting childish by saying, "I'm staying here until I hear from You God"? Maybe this whole idea was foolish. If God wanted to speak to me, I didn't have to find a secluded place in Connecticut. He's God and could do whatever He wanted, wherever He wanted to do it.

I didn't sleep well that night as doubts that God would ever speak to me raced through my mind. Who was I kidding? I was a felon on parole. There were plenty of good candidates for a pastoral ministry. I was beginning to disqualify myself from ever hearing from God. If He did speak, He'd probably say, "Rejected." It was Sunday morning. If I wanted to "hear" from God I should perhaps be sitting in church with my family. As I sat there with feelings of despair, God's presence began to take over. Despondency fled my mind as a fresh wind of hope rose up within me. God was going to speak to me and I knew it. I opened the door, stepped out of my Gremlin and entered the sanctuary of His Presence. Lyrics from an old hymn, "In the Garden" accurately defined the moment. *"He speaks, and the sound of His voice, is so sweet the birds hush their singing."* Without an audible sound, I knew God had clearly spoken to my heart. I had finally heard His seemingly elusive WORD. God was indeed calling me into pastoral ministry. The doubt that had gripped me quickly vanished as a peaceful confirmation settled into my heart. It was going to happen. How? I didn't know, but somehow I was at peace that it was going to happen!

It was still early Sunday morning and if I hurried back there would be enough time to get home, shower, and make it to church. I could hardly wait to get back and tell my wife and Pastor Farrington. Irene shared the excitement with me, although neither one of us fully understood what it meant to be "called". We decided not to reveal our news to anyone in church until first sharing it with Pastor Farrington. It wasn't until Tuesday morning that I finally had my opportunity to sit down with him and reveal my confirmation. With brimming excitement, I said to him, "Pastor Farrington, I have some exciting news to tell you. God has called me to become a pastor." He sat there with a huge grin on his face and I knew that my news was a joy to his heart. After a moment of silence he said, "I knew that Phil. I've known it for years. God revealed it to me when I was your Chaplain in Attica." As my "father in the faith" Pastor Farrington's validation was important to me and upon receiving it I could not have been more elated. "But Pastor, if you knew this for all these years, why didn't you tell me?" Again he looked my way with a huge grin on his face and said, "My son, it wasn't my business to tell you! It was God's. You had to hear it from Him. If I told you God had a call on your life you might have questioned your call. When ministry work becomes challenging (and it will) you would be tempted to blame me for leading you down the wrong path. Now you will make it through those difficult times because you know He has called you into this work. Never forget it. You must know that you know God has called you!"

# Chapter Thirty

## Straddle of Indecision

*"A person's steps are directed by the Lord. How then can anyone understand their own way?" (Proverbs 20:24)*

With Pastor Farrington's confirmation, I felt like a young wild stallion let out of the gate. I wasn't sure what to do next but I was eager to find out. In a few days Pastor Farrington, with all his wisdom, sat me down and began instructing me in the way I should go. His direction was basic yet very helpful. He reminded me that the achievement of pastoring a church someday would take much more than desire. Perseverance and determination would be required of me. The confirmation was the easy part; the fulfillment was up to me. He reminded me that the most important factor in seeing it come to pass was my relationship with the Lord. "This is a calling from God much more than it is a vocational choice." He said spending time in prayer and reading (studying) my Bible would be of paramount importance in preparing me for the days ahead. Before leaving his office that morning Pastor Farrington had scheduled a personal appointment for me with our church's district superintendent in nearby Massachusetts.

The superintendent was very happy to hear about my call and was eager to get me started down the road. He assigned me to a supervising pastor who would guide me along the way. There were numerous applications to fill out, forms to sign, and appointments to keep. We met regularly (twice a month) to make sure I was staying on course. I was encouraged to go back to school; so in September of 1984 I enrolled at Providence College in Rhode Island.

Life was busy with family, church, college, work, and the required meetings with my supervisor. I really enjoyed these meetings. I was often reminded of the call upon my life and encouraged to stay the course. I successfully completed my fall courses and in January 1985 I began another semester. Although my activities in church were keeping me busy I was chomping away at the bit to stand behind a pulpit on a regular basis in fulfillment of my call. The prophet Jeremiah described my feelings well when he declared, *".....His WORD is in my heart like a fire, a fire shut up in my bones. I am weary of holding it in; indeed, I cannot." (Jeremiah 20:9)*

Waiting is never easy, especially if one is waiting for something of enormous desire. My heart was saying, "Be patient" while my flesh was ready to set up a pulpit on my front yard. How long will it take? I remember asking that question to my supervising pastor and I also remember his answer. "Phil, I can see your eagerness and your desire to pastor a church. Our denomination does not always move as fast as we think it should. Some have waited as long as ten years. Be patient and stay the course." As I drove home that day I remember feeling the air had been let out of my balloon. I was deflated. TEN YEARS! Although I was only 37 years old, I felt I'd be an old man in 10 years.

Almost miraculously, in April of 1985 I received a call from a prison ministry in Orlando, Florida searching for a full-time director of their residential program. Somehow through a series of associations my name came up as a possible candidate. I found myself talking with (the late) Rev. Frank Constantino, the founder of the Christian-based Orlando Bridge residential program for men getting out of prison. He talked for quite some time, explaining what the responsibilities of the director would be. To my ears it didn't sound like a residential director's job. It sounded like they needed a pastor.

# *Straddle of Indecision*

Could this phone call be God's leading? Would I soon be moving to Florida? "Think it over Phil! Pray about it. The position may well be yours if you want it. You have time to decide but we'd like to have the new director hired by early summer." "Thank you Frank," I responded, "I'm sure we'll talk again real soon." Would my family and I be moving to Florida in two short months? My spirit was immediately lifted until I shared my good news with my wife Irene. She reminded me of a condition over which we both had felt strongly. "I thought God was calling you to pastor a church in New England not Florida?" she said, "Are you sure about this?" Frank was right! We needed to pray about it. Although we were still living in Rhode Island we began seeing cars with Florida license plates everywhere. "Could this be a sign from God?" Or was God indeed calling me to New England? "Lord, help us make the right decision!" *"He (GOD) will instruct them in the ways they should choose." (Psalm 25:12)*

Some good news did arrive to our home on May 26, 1985, with the birth of our precious daughter Cheryl. Despite our joy, time was going by and a decision still needed to be made. The next couple of weeks were nerve racking. The Orlando Ministry contacted me several more times, wanting to know if I had decided to accept their offer. I was reminded that time was running out.

On Saturday Morning June 29th I attended a prayer breakfast with some of our area pastors. One of them noticed my troubled countenance and asked, "What's the problem Phil? You look troubled. Is everything alright this morning?" A number of others had also taken notice. I proceeded to explain my dilemma and how the thought of ten more years was so very overwhelming. I also explained that the Orlando offer had to be settled soon. I had felt rather confident that God was indeed calling me to New England but now I was confused. Maybe God was calling me to move to Florida for a few years and prepare me for my pastorate in New England? God does work in strange ways at times.

I was sure each of the pastors at the meeting that morning had their own story to share concerning important decisions in their lives. I had been asking God to guide my steps and now it was time to remove myself from the straddle of indecision. One of the pastors encouraged me to pray and take a step of faith. Pastor Ken boldly proclaimed, "Ten years is nothing to God. If He wanted you to be a pastor by next Sunday it would not be too difficult for Him to do." The overall consensus that morning was God indeed had a call on my life. *"....being confident of this, that He who began a good work in you will carry it on to completion until the day of Christ Jesus." (Philippians 1:6)* I went home that Saturday morning filled with hopeful anticipation that God would soon be leading me to a place of correct decision. The next morning at our church's Worship service I thanked God for the peace that was within me.

On Sunday evening June 30th I received another call from Frank Constantino. It was my time of decision. Frank understood my reluctance but he needed an answer. "Here's what I'll do," Frank said. "Book a flight for Monday. We will cover all your expenses. Come down and see for yourself what this ministry entails. Spend a week with us. I'll even take you to see the "Big Rat at Disney" (that's what he called Mickey Mouse). Make it a family vacation if you'd like but get here as soon as possible. If you don't want the job, I have someone else waiting to take it." Dependent upon getting time off from work I agreed to be there as soon as possible. Since I was no longer under parole supervision I was able to leave the state without first gaining the state's approval. I was getting ready to take a step of faith. Before turning in for the night, Irene and I prayed that God would stop us if the Orlando assignment was not from Him.

# Chapter Thirty-One

## It was Prophetic!

*"For prophecy never had its origin in the human will, but prophets, though human, spoke from God as they were carried along by the Holy Spirit." (2Peter 1:21)*

On Monday morning, July 1st I went to work as usual. I worked as a Custom-Color Technician blending pigments and dyes to make various color fabrics. The job was a demanding one and many who had tried the job in the past had failed. Matching "true color" is a task that requires unique color perception ability. It took precision measuring and a good-eye to satisfy the color demands of our customers. I noticed my supervisor Carlos wasn't very busy so I asked for a moment of his time. "I need to take a few days off for personal reasons. Is it possible for me to take the rest of this week off?" I had a good working relationship with Carlos and he greatly appreciated my satisfactory and ambitious efforts. I was not only caught up on my work, I was actually weeks ahead on orders. With this in mind he replied, "No problem Phil. As a matter of fact you can have the next two weeks off. Finish off your morning assignments and you can leave at noon."

I immediately called my wife with the good news. "Irene, I've got the time off from work. Please call the airport and book my flight. If possible I'd like to leave tonight." She agreed to arrange it. By 10am that morning she had my flight booked and was packing my luggage for the trip. Since Cheryl was just a little more than a month old, Irene decided not to make this business and pleasure trip with me. "Thanks Honey. There's still one more thing you can do for me. Please make a phone call to Orlando and let them know what time my flight arrives. They said they would have someone pick me up at the airport." "No problem" she replied. "I'll call them and then finish packing your bags. See you in a couple hours."

At approximately 11am as I was finishing up my morning work assignment, Irene called me and said, "You're not going to believe who just called. I was getting ready to call Florida when the phone rang. The church district superintendent has just called and said it was urgent that he talk to you as soon as possible. He said he had a church that he wanted you to serve." Neither one of us knew what he meant by "serve". Was God possibly stopping us from moving to Florida? I asked Irene to cancel my flight and I'd call our superintendant as soon as I arrived home.

By 3pm, Irene and I were sitting in District Headquarters near Holden, Massachusetts. The Superintendent cordially welcomed us into his office and said, "Phil, tell me your story. How were you born-again? Why did you go to prison? When did you get out? Why do you think you have a call on your life?" For the next hour or two I proceeded to tell him the story of my conversion, incarceration, and why I believed God had a call on my life. He listened intently and asked only a few pertinent questions along the way. After I had finished sharing my life experience with him he said, "Phil, there's a church in Fitchburg, Massachusetts that's in need of a pastor and I think you'd be a perfect fit for that church. I'd like to assign you to the pastorate position as soon as possible." Was I dreaming? Then I remembered the words that Pastor Ken boldly proclaimed to me just two days earlier, "Ten years is nothing to God. If He wanted you to be a pastor by next Sunday it would not be too difficult for Him to do." Irene and I were speechless. Did we hear him right? Did he actually say, "Pastorate"? He unfolded a map and showed us where Fitchburg was located. "I am ready to assign you the position but there's one stipulation. You must meet with the church council in Fitchburg and share your story with them. If they accept you, I will officially appoint you to the church. I wouldn't want to assign you there if the people are strongly resistant to an ex-prisoner being their pastor. It wouldn't be fair to you or them." By 5pm, we were headed back home to Woonsocket; our mind grappling to understand the events of the day.

Two days later, on Wednesday July 3rd, Irene and I and our newborn baby Cheryl headed for Fitchburg, Massachusetts to meet with the church council at 7pm. When I was in Attica prison the Lord first spoke to my heart concerning a church in New England. It was then that I had a vision in my mind's eye of how the church looked, a typical New England Church with its bell tower overlooking the community. As we approached the church, I looked up and there it was; the image I had so vividly seen in Attica some seven to eight years earlier. Small tears of confirmation formed under my eyelids and rolled down my cheek, and I knew this was the right place.

We introduced ourselves to the board as they did the same, and the meeting began. They were extremely polite; I was extremely nervous. "Tell us all about yourself. We hear you have quite a testimony to share." For the next hour I shared my testimony. I did not hold anything back.

My conviction, my incarceration, all of it was laid out before them. When I finished speaking, Anita, one of the council members, got excited and said, "I was watching *The 700 Club* on TV this morning. The guest speaker was a pastor who had previously spent time in prison." She said she prayed for a man like that to be our pastor. I told them that I didn't have any pastoral experience yet I was confident of my call and believed that I could meet their needs.

After asking Irene a few questions they excused us from their meeting to allow a council discussion. "Brad will give you a tour of the church property including the parsonage then bring you back in about 30 minutes. We might have a few more questions to ask you. Then you can go home." Brad told us that it was highly unlikely a decision would be made that evening. They'd probably get back to us within a week or two. Their brief closed-door meeting ended as Irene and I were escorted back into the room. When we entered they all stood up with their hands extended gesturing a desire to shake our hands. I expected them to say "Thank you for your time. We'll be getting back to you." Instead, in unison they said, "Congratulations, the board has unanimously voted. We strongly believe God has sent you to us." I accepted their offer and at that moment I officially became their Pastor. The financial package offered by the church board was $100 per week plus a housing allowance that included a home for our family in the church parsonage. It wasn't much but it was all we needed. All this took place within four days since Pastor Ken said "If God wanted you to be a pastor **by next Sunday** it would not be too difficult for Him to do." His words proved to be prophetic. As we drove home that evening, we could hardly believe all that had transpired within a few short days. Although I was void of any formal pastoral training, the calling superseded the credentialing. *"With man this is impossible, but with God all things are possible." (Matthew 19:26)*

# It was Prophetic

The next couple of weeks would be extremely busy preparing for our move to Fitchburg. Most of the transition was smooth and relatively uneventful but there would be another offer that we faced attempting to lure us away from God's plan. Although I had the next two weeks off from work, I still had the responsibility of giving my two-week notice. When I told my boss I was moving to Massachusetts to become a pastor he looked at me and asked a rather personal question. "How much are they paying you?" Why was he asking me such a question? Although I did not have to answer such a personal question I said, "$100 per week!" He gazed my way for a moment then said, "Are you crazy? You can't live on that." I understood his concern. $5,200 per year was barely enough money to put food on the table for a family of five, with two still in diapers.

Although our decision to leave was already settled in our hearts, he then proceeded to tell me that his position was soon opening up because he was moving up the ladder in the company. I was told that I was being considered for promotion to his assignment, which had the potential of offering a considerable increase in salary and fringe benefits. Upon sharing this news with Irene, her immediate response was, "No way! That's a lure from the enemy. God's called you to be a pastor and that's that. We don't even have to pray about it. We already know what the answer is. Now let's get back to packing; we have a lot to do." Irene is seldom as bold as she was that day. She was absolutely right. Satan was attempting to distract us from the will of God for our lives and we both knew it!

At the end of two weeks we had somehow managed to pack our U-Haul rental truck and relocate our family of five to our new home in Fitchburg, Massachusetts, Our journey of faith was about to begin. Through the miraculous hand of God I was now a pastor and Irene was now a pastor's wife.

# *Twice Convicted*

"Pastor," someone standing near me called out. "Pastor," they called again, "Pastor, do you have a minute?" I vividly remember the first time someone called me by that title. At first I ignored their call not realizing they were speaking to me. I quickly apologized for my hesitant response. Ten years earlier I was an inmate behind a prison wall; now I was fulfilling God's call preaching behind a pastor's pulpit. I was learning of the many responsibilities that encompass the pastoral calling. A phone call or a knock on the door could take place at any time night or day. I soon realized that my on the job training was a 24-7 calling and we considered it all to be my greatest ever of job promotions.

Like that of many young pastors some of my earlier sermons were theologically askew. I thank God for a congregation that tolerated my inexperience with tremendous amounts of God's love and patience. I did my best to officiate professionally at wedding ceremonies, preside at funerals, visit terminally sick patients in hospitals, perform baptisms, baby dedications, and so much more while still being wet behind the ears. In His great love, God elected to entrust me with responsibility for the care of His precious sheep. Jesus said, *"Take care of my sheep". (John 21:16b)*

# Epilogue

*"For I know the plans I have for you," declares the Lord, "plans to prosper you and not to harm you, plans to give you hope and a future." (Jeremiah 29:11)*

During the early years of my pastorate I sometimes felt like I was being stretched beyond my ability. I grew to a far better understanding that God's power flows best through vessels that have been emptied of their own strength and capabilities. There were many times when I cried out to God for His help to care for others. Please don't misunderstand me. I was experiencing great personal joy and satisfaction in fulfilling God's call upon my life. There were many hurting people, but there also were many mighty warriors of the faith that God had placed around me. I seldom felt that I was alone.

Fitchburg, Massachusetts turned out to be a wonderful place to live; a middle size city with a population of approximately 40,000. Along with shepherding the flock at our church, there were ample opportunities for service within our city. Like most towns across America, it had its trouble spots. Poverty, drug traffic, prostitution, alcoholism, homelessness, gang activity, and crime are all part of a typical inner-city. Cleghorn, a section of Fitchburg that was once the pride of the city had over the years deteriorated to become the inner-city trouble spot of our region. From the late 70's through the early years of 2000, the reputation of Cleghorn was one of trouble. Many people did their best to avoid going to or through Cleghorn. It badly needed a community church, but none was to be found.

As I drove into Cleghorn one afternoon my heart was troubled by what I saw and soon God began revealing His heart to me for these people. My concern for Cleghorn continued to deepen until finally after five years I submitted a formal letter of resignation at the church where I was serving.

I eventually found myself opening up a storefront church in the heart of Cleghorn. I recall vividly the first day I went to look at the building that would eventually become our church. A small group of us did a walk-through of the storefront building to see if it would meet our needs. It wasn't much of a place but we all felt that with a little elbow grease, fresh paint, and a whole lot of vision, this building would be a great church building. While we were inspecting the place, a thunderstorm was passing by outside. As we waited for the storm to clear we prayed and asked God to bless our efforts to reach the community with His love. The storm cleared and as we walked outside a brilliant rainbow arched across the street, and as we watched, the rainbow over Fairmount Street became a double rainbow. We believed it to be a sign from God that we indeed were venturing out into His will. The call to reach the people of Cleghorn with the love of God became etched in our hearts that night.

Over the years we reached out in this location to multitudes of people with the love of God. A free clothing ministry, food pantry, homeless shelter, outdoor services, and free lunch program all became part of our outreach. Our doors opened each morning at approximately 7 o'clock and soon dozens of children along with a few parents would enter in for free donuts and a drink before going off to school. One of the most impacting outreach activities was led by Rev. Esther and Peter Plastridge. Free food, activities, and children's ministries were their specialty. Their "Friday-Nite Live" ministry to the children led to hundreds of them making personal commitments to Christ.

At one point in my pastorate an opening for a chaplain in one of Massachusetts State prisons was presented to me. One Friday evening I was invited to speak to a group of inmates in the nearby Lancaster Correctional Facility. I ministered to the men that night and after the service ended the chaplain informed me that he was leaving his current chaplain's position to work at another state prison. As a result, the Lancaster prison would be without a chaplain. He strongly believed that it was God's will for me to replace him and become the next chaplain. After much prayer, I accepted the chaplain's position. As one might imagine, my incarceration in Attica proved to be tremendously beneficial in ministering to other inmates.

As time went on both the church in Cleghorn and the prison ministry had become more demanding of my time. No longer could I juggle my schedule enough to be effective at both. After tenure of seven years and much prayer I realized that I could better serve our church by relinquishing the prison chaplain's assignment to someone else; someone who would give inmates the quality time they needed.

Throughout over 25 years of ministry God's provision remained constant. When I first responded to the call of God upon my life for $100 a week, God was faithful to meet all of our needs and has continued to do so throughout our lives. Sometimes, in our small church, weeks would pass without any pastoral pay yet God was always faithful to put food on our table, gas in our tank, and a few dollars in our wallets. The necessary things of this world will be provided to those who trust in Him. I never could have imagined the blessings that would later befall us in our walk; a trip to the Holy Land to more deeply embed our Scriptural understanding, four (4) mission's trips to Haiti, and also an invitation to minister at a church in England. *"But seek first His kingdom and His righteousness and all these things will be given to you as well." (Matthew 6:33)*

It is my prayerful hope that after reading this book you might have a greater desire for a stronger Godly presence in your own life. In my case, He has forgiven me, mended me, and used me for His purposes and he can do the same for you. He changes lives, heals the broken hearted, and sets the captives free. His abundance of mercy and grace are available to all who call upon the name of the Lord. For those who already know of His love, I pray that your walk with Him might become strengthened through the testimonies shared in this book.

If you're one who has never opened up your heart to a loving God, my prayer is that this book will beckon you to do so. As a sinner guilty of manslaughter, my walk was started with a simple heartfelt prayer. I now offer one similar to that which I recited and encourage you to join in such a prayer.

*Dear Lord, I admit that I am a sinner.*
*I have lived selfishly and I am truly sorrowful*
*I repent and I accept your forgiveness*
*I invite you into my heart*
*I believe you died on the cross for me, to save me.*
*You did for me what I could not do for myself.*
*In faith, I ask you to reveal your plans for my life*
*Thank you for coming into my heart.*
*Help me daily to live a life that is pleasing to you.*
*In Jesus Name,* ***AMEN***

If you just prayed this simple prayer from the sincerity of your heart God has forgiven and accepted you into His family. You have been born again. Congratulations on your new birth. *"Therefore, if anyone is in Christ, He is a new creation; the old has gone, the new has come!" (2Corinthians 5:17)* Now go ahead and live life to its fullest.

If you have a friend that is a Christian call them and share your experience. Ask them to help you discover the plan God has for your life. Find yourself a good Bible believing church and begin your journey. I would love to hear from you and celebrate your decision with you. I'm on "Facebook" or you can contact me at the following address:

Philip J. Cebula
245 Walton Street
Fitchburg, MA. 01420

twiceconvicted@gmail.com